DON'T LOOK BACK, YOU'LL TRIP OVER

Also by Michael Caine:

The Elephant to Hollywood
Blowing the Bloody Doors Off
Deadly Game

DON'T LOOK BACK, YOU'LL TRIP OVER

My Guide to Life

MICHAEL CAINE

IN CONVERSATION WITH MATTHEW D'ANCONA

HODDER &
STOUGHTON

First published in Great Britain in 2024 by Hodder & Stoughton Limited
An Hachette UK company

1

Copyright © Michael Caine 2024

The right of Michael Caine to be identified as the Author of the Work has been
asserted by him in accordance with the Copyright, Designs and Patents Act 1988.

A CIP catalogue record for this title is available from the British Library

Hardback ISBN 9781399739979
Trade Paperback ISBN 9781399739986
ebook ISBN 9781399739993

Typeset in Celeste by Hewer Text UK Ltd, Edinburgh
Printed and bound in Great Britain by Clays Ltd, Elcograf S.p.A.

Hodder & Stoughton policy is to use papers that are natural, renewable
and recyclable products and made from wood grown in sustainable
forests. The logging and manufacturing processes are expected to
conform to the environmental regulations of the country of origin.

Hodder & Stoughton Limited
Carmelite House
50 Victoria Embankment
London EC4Y 0DZ

The authorised representative in the EEA is Hachette Ireland, 8 Castlecourt
Centre, Dublin 15, D15 XTP3, Ireland (email: info@hbgi.ie)

www.hodder.co.uk

For Niki, Natasha, Taylor, Ally, Miles, Zac and Teddy

CONTENTS

PREFACE

I AM ALWAYS ASKED questions – by fans, by other actors and friends, by my grandchildren. They want to know how I've lasted so long, how I handle fame, why I chose to do some of my films, which films, directors and actors I like best and so forth.

They also want to know what makes me tick, what makes me get up in the morning in my nineties, and whether I'll ever retire. (The answer to that one, by the way, is 'No!'). These days, everyone is looking for what I'm told are called 'life hacks': unexpected solutions to everyday problems. Often, the answer is simple, though it isn't necessarily easy.

Over a long life, I've learned a lot and had the opportunity to reflect. I've seen a new generation grow up, among them my own grandchildren, facing the world with all its challenges and problems.

I've also never done a book of interviews. So I asked my friend Matt d'Ancona to do the journalistic honours and lob some questions my way.

What follows is the distillation of many hours of conversation during 2023 and 2024, over lunch, dinner and countless cups of coffee. The more we talked, the clearer the main themes became and the more the key lessons stood out. I have loved writing memoirs in the past, but this was a very different – and fun – way of thinking about what it all meant.

If you're wondering about the book's title, it's something I often say to my grandchildren: 'Don't look back, you'll trip over.' Of course, that doesn't mean you can't think about what you've done, what you've experienced and the lessons you've learned.

You absolutely should – and a lot of this book is about just that. What it *does* mean is that you should keep your eyes fixed firmly forward, even when you're learning from those lessons. Understanding your past is very different from being stuck in it.

I've loved my life and career but, as you'll see, I am even more interested in what's going on today and what might happen tomorrow. Which is why this book is dedicated to my daughters, my grandchildren and to Matt's sons.

I have been helped by many people along the way, and I hope that what I've learned helps you, whatever you do – or dream of doing. There are many ways of being a star.

My own dreams have come true because of my beloved wife, Shakira, and the life we have built together. I thank her from the bottom of my heart.

Enjoy!

Michael Caine,
London, September 2024

'Pay attention, there'll be a test at the end.'

1

Are You Ready to Fall Through the Door?

So, let's begin at the beginning. To adapt a famous line from one of your most famous movies: what's it all about, Michael?

Well, we'll get to that. But you're right to start at the beginning. Because I've never forgotten my roots, and nobody should. They define you – though they shouldn't limit you.

And you started out around the Elephant and Castle, in south London?

Yes, just south of the river – though I was actually born in Rotherhithe, which is in east London, in 1933. Very much a working-class background, and, like everyone then, my childhood was shaped by the war. My dad worked as a porter at the fish market and my mum was a charlady. We lived in a prefab.

What happened to you during the war?

We were evacuated. My younger brother Stanley and I were split up at first, but then Mum and the two of us ended up in a village called North Runcton in Norfolk, which is on the east coast of England.

That must have been pretty disorienting.

Yes, but at the time you don't think about it that way. It really helped that my mum knew how to handle the situation, even though she was obviously very upset by the whole thing. When my dad went to off to Dunkirk, an Army lorry came round on a Monday morning to pick him up in the village. The truth is, we didn't know if he was going to come back. A lot of men didn't, after all. So we stood there, and my mother was crying as he headed off round the corner in the village.

Then – and I'll never forget this – she turned to me and Stanley, we were six and three, and she said, 'Now you've got to look after me.' And she made little men of us instantly. She wasn't being unkind. The opposite, actually. She was giving us something to aim for, if you like, and to take our minds off our own sadness. A new role in life to make us focus on getting through the challenges ahead.

So it felt less like a burden than a task that could make sense of what you and your brother were facing?

Exactly. Everybody needs purpose in life, even little kids. It helps a confused young boy if he knows that he's got to step up and help his mum. Takes his mind off the other stuff. And

I think everyone needs to be given a sense of purpose, or to find one for themselves.

At all ages?

Very much so. You don't do young people any favours by not teaching them self-reliance or by denying them responsibilities. I don't mean by neglecting them, that's a terrible thing to do to a child. I mean showing them love by encouraging them to stand on their own two feet and to be all that they can be. You're there to catch them if they fall, but you want them to grow as individuals. I think it's at the heart of parenting, actually. Love, a roof over their head, and a bit of a roadmap in life.

What did you make of life in the countryside?

Oh, it was a stroke of luck. In a weird way, the Second World War was the best thing that ever happened to me – certainly in terms of my health, because it got me away from all the pollution and industrial filth around Bermondsey. I basically lived on a farm for six years. All the food was what we nowadays call organic and so we ate really well. I had rickets as a kid, but I'm sure that all that good country air and food accounts for the fact that I ended up being six foot two.

So you made the best of a terrible situation?

More than that, I think. You have to come to terms with what your life is right now, and what it can be in the future. Of course, when you're a kid you never spell it out like that. But you can have an instinct.

One thing is to look out for the people who appreciate you and will help you. I was very fortunate at the little elementary school in the village – there was a teacher called Miss Linton. She was probably about sixty at the time, very kindly. She spotted some sort of potential in me and encouraged me to read and to do maths. She used poker to teach me maths! It was because of her that I took the London County Council scholarship – this would have been in 1944, I think – and off I went to Hackney Downs Grammar School. Harold Pinter went there, too, actually.

What other mentors did you have when you were growing up?

Well, someone I owe a lot to is a guy called the Reverend Jimmy Butterworth – can't have been more than five feet tall – and he was a Methodist minister from up north who had created this club called Clubland on the Walworth Road from scratch in the 1930s. And that was a very important place for me, sort of an island full of possibilities.

How so?

I knew from quite early on that I wanted to be in the movies. You see, if you're talking about mentors, you have to include the people you might never meet – in my case, Humphrey Bogart and Marlon Brando. Actually, I *did* meet Marlon many years later, in Park Lane, but only for a few minutes. We were both out drinking! And Shakira and I got to know Bogart's widow, Lauren Bacall – or Betty, as we knew her – very well.

But that's not really the point. You can have mentors in your imagination, as well as in real life. You can see someone on the big screen, or the football pitch, or being a famous scientist, and say, 'That's what I'd like to be.' Even if other people tell you it's a ridiculous ambition. Only *you* get to choose your dreams.

What did you admire about those two actors in particular?

Well, I think Brando in *On the Waterfront* (1954) is just one of the greatest screen performances ever. And Bogart is incredible because you can't really tell he's acting. He wasn't tall, dark and handsome and I looked at him and thought, well, he became a movie star, why can't I?

I'm not specifically a film noir actor – nobody is any more – but Bogart's film noir work was a big influence on me. I try to be self-contained on screen. I don't do much, if that makes sense, because real people don't do much. Over the years, I've learned a lot about cameras and what they can do. You never stop learning. And I started, without knowing it, just by watching Bogart on screen.

And, of course, Leslie Howard was another of my movie mentors, particularly because he was fair-haired like me. People probably remember him most today for *Gone with the Wind* (1939), which is still one of my top ten movies of all times.

So movies were more than just entertainment for you?

Well, it *was* entertainment, of course. How can you watch *Casablanca* (1942) and not be swept into a different world? Or *The Treasure of the Sierra Madre* (1948)? Or *The Maltese Falcon* (1941)?

But it meant more to me than just escapism. I went to the Trocadero up at the Elephant and Castle – it was a huge movie house, long gone now, the 'Troc' we used to call it. I started going to the cinema, and pretty soon it felt like I lived there. I was so impressed by it. It was never the stage I was drawn to first and foremost. It was always the movies. I thought it was magical. It made me want to be someone, and start thinking that I could be.

But first you had to learn to be a stage actor? As a means to an end?

Well, yes. I mean, I didn't have much choice, really. Actually, it was girls rather than ambition that led me to acting in the first place. I was at Clubland one evening, when I was eleven, and I was going up to the basketball on the roof. There was a door with two windows in it, and I looked in, and there were all the prettiest girls in the club. I didn't know what was going on in there, but it certainly interested me. And one day I was looking through the door at this girl I really liked, leaning on it – and I fell in on the floor, like Buster Keaton!

A star is born?

Everyone has to start somewhere, I suppose. So there I was on the ground, and the head lady got me up and asked me if I wanted to join. I quickly said I was on my way up to the basketball court. But she said, 'Look, I want you to join, and I'll tell you why. We don't have a single boy in this group, it's all girls.' So I signed up there and then.

Of course, back in those days, most lads thought that taking an interest in theatre meant you were gay. Well, I couldn't care less what they thought. I wanted to be around the best-looking girls. And, pretty soon, I realised that acting itself was something I might just be good at. I played a robot in a play, my first play, and afterwards the producer came up to me and said, 'Robots don't show emotions – and you were perfect!'

A funny start – like most starts, I guess.

So the moral of the story is: be ready for the accident to happen?

Exactly. You never know when you're going to fall through the right door. If I hadn't fallen through that door, I would never have gone to Hollywood, or won two Oscars, or had all the unbelievable good fortune I've had.

Another minor, but important factor: I've always been a natural observer because very early on, my dad bought a television and I started watching that and I thought, I could do that. Or to put it another way, I couldn't think of anything *else* I could do. Which amounted to the same thing.

But you were only a teenager. Did you have any inkling of how far acting might take you?

Oh, not at that point, no. I *did* wonder whether this was a way I could make some money eventually. I don't mean get rich, and certainly not famous. I just mean get some money in my pocket, so I'd have some freedom. My feeling was, 'I don't want to be confined financially, I don't want my horizons to be limited.'

That work ethic – it's a thread running through your career. How did you stay out of trouble when you were young and keep your focus?

The Elephant and Castle was full of gangs when I was growing up. But I wasn't ever drawn to that kind of lifestyle, I wanted to be an individual and do my own thing. I'm not saying that people shouldn't join groups or belong to things they enjoy. Collaboration is vital to a happy life. But my experience has been that you should always start with your own beliefs rather than follow the herd.

I looked at the gangs – I didn't want to be dishonest, or to steal things, or hit people. I knew a lot of the gangsters; a couple of them were my uncles. But I didn't want to follow their path at all. I didn't want any involvement with the police or prison, none of that at all. I wanted real freedom.

You've played gangsters in great movies – Jack Carter in Get Carter *(1971) and Denny Mortwell in* Mona Lisa *(1986). Did you draw on that experience?*

Oh, of course. You always draw on your experience when you're playing a part. But that's not me at all. I hate violence and bully-ing. It's called acting for a reason! No, I played by the rules.

Speaking of rules – how did you find National Service?

It's pretty hard to exaggerate the impact it had on me. Look, I'm ninety-one and, seventy years on, I can still remember it and the effect it had on me. That's a measure of what the ex-perience was like.

I mean, just imagine: eighteen-year-old boys in south London, all of us, suddenly in uniform and being sent overseas. I was sent to Germany as part of the occupation force in Berlin first and then it was on to Korea for the second year. It turned me from a boy into a man, it was the start of adulthood.

What did it teach you?

You have to be self-reliant, but also put your trust in your mates when you're out on patrol. So you're learning how to be an individual *and* part of a group with a shared purpose; that's invaluable, in any walk of life. I was just an ordinary private soldier, I wasn't anything special, I was one of 500 others. We just had to get up every night and fight the Chinese army – the Chinese government had sent half a million troops to help North Korea – it was a bugger.

That's quite a big deal at any age.

Yes, I suppose so, but when you're in the thick of things you just get on with it. Looking back, the memories are very sharp, which tells you how powerful an experience it was. I remember one night me and six other guys were out on patrol in the Samichon Valley, right on the line between North and South Korea. And we knew the enemy were close. We were all bloody scared, of course. But we made it past them, and went towards the Chinese line, and then turned left and headed back.

Just as a little bonus, we all got bitten by the bleeding mosquitoes. But let's put it this way – that was better than being shot by the Chinese.

Years later, you and Brendan Fraser starred in a terrific version of Graham Greene's The Quiet American *(2002), which is all about the beginnings of the Vietnam conflict. Actually, that was one of your Oscar nominations, for playing the journalist Thomas Fowler. Did making that movie stir those memories of brushes with death on patrol?*

Oh, very much so, of course. They were two different wars, but they had things in common. I was a huge admirer of Graham Greene, actually. I had already starred in an adaptation of another of his novels, *The Honorary Consul* (1983). It was set in Argentina and filmed in Mexico. I played Charley Fortnum, a sozzled British consul, alongside Bob Hoskins, who became a great friend, and Richard Gere, who was quite shy but a lovely guy.

Thing is, Greene didn't like the film. But he came up to me in the Connaught one evening and said that he had really enjoyed my performance. Which goes to show, you *should* meet your heroes!

Would you bring back National Service?

I would. I believe in National Service for young people. I don't mean that they should go to war or be in the line of fire – nothing like that. I'd make it for six months rather than two years like it used to be. But being eighteen years old and serving in the Forces for your country – it teaches you a lot. How to live and how to sort yourself out. You grow up.

But it would be different to your experience, wouldn't it?

Yes, because the world has changed. I did my service not long after the Second World War. Today, things are much more complicated and, in a way, more frightening. I look at the news and see all this death in Ukraine and the Middle East and elsewhere – I am not for a minute suggesting sending young British men off to die or to be in combat. I believe in peace very strongly.

But I also think that military training is a good thing in itself. It sands the edges off you as a young person and prepares you for the rough and tumble of life. That's got to be useful for you and for all those you interact with in the years that follow. I think we've lost sight of the fact that self-discipline actually frees you up to do whatever you want with your life. It might seem an odd thing to say, but National Service is a liberating experience in the long run.

So discipline gives you some of the tools that make you ready when opportunity strikes. When did it strike next for you?

Well, it's a bit like falling through the door at the youth club. Except this time it was a chance meeting. After National Service, I came back and I didn't have any money. I needed a job and I had no skills. So I ended up working in Bermondsey, packing trucks with stuff.

There was this guy working with me, must have been around seventy. And one day, he took me aside and said, 'Maurice' – I was still called Maurice Micklewhite back then – 'what are you doing working here, Maurice, what do you want to do with your life? Do you really want to pack bleeding butter into lorries like me?' He said, 'My life is nearly over, but you're twenty, you're just stepping out, what do you want to do?'

I was a bit taken aback, but I thought, well, it's a fair question. So I said, 'Well, I want to be an actor, actually – but I don't know how to go about it.'

And he said, 'Well, it's your lucky day, because *I do*.'

What did you think?

I thought he must be mad. But I thought I'd see what he said, anyway. I mean, what did I have to lose? So I said, 'You do?'

And he carries on, 'Yes. You go to Leicester Square and in one corner of Leicester Square is a theatre called the Hippodrome, and opposite the tube station, you cross the road, you walk up to Tottenham Court Road, and eventually you'll come to a newsagent called Solosy's.'

I said, 'Yes, I know that newsagent, as it happens, I buy the *Evening Standard* in there sometimes.'

He said, 'Well, go in there, go right to the back, past the regular newspapers, and there's a paper called *The Stage*. Buy it, ignore all the stuff at the front, and go straight to the back page and it's for stage managers and small parts that pay £5 a week.'

I said, 'Okay, I'll do it.'

And did it work?

I bought the paper, found an ad, went for an interview and, before I knew it, I was an assistant stage manager with a small repertory company in Horsham, Sussex.

Just like that.

Yes, but the point is that I was ready to hear what he had to say, and to act upon it. I was hungry and he spotted that. If I hadn't wanted to make it as an actor, I would have just nodded politely and forgotten all about his advice. But I was on the look-out. Luck only works when you're ready to take advantage of it. Otherwise, it's just wasted.

And not every conversation like that pans out, does it?

Absolutely not. And it wasn't as if all the lights suddenly turned green. I was working very hard – half the time I wasn't even acting, I was shopping for props or meals, and to save money I'd always get an extra one for me. I did almost 1,000 auditions before I was thirty. I played dozens of parts in rep companies and did more one-line roles on telly than I care to mention. It was seriously hard work and often amounted to one rejection after another. But in rep I had a place where I could really learn my trade – come hell or high water.

Why was rep so useful? I mean, what you really wanted to do was movies.

That's true. But I also realised that I could pick up invaluable skills in rep.

And you did. What was rep theatre like?

It was a pretty brutal conveyor belt. I was doing one play a week in the evening, but also learning the lines for next week in the daytime – plus rehearsals. And the habit of learning lines was *invaluable.* You read about so many big movie stars who have had to read off dummy cards on set because they just can't or won't learn their lines. But, by the time I got into making films, it was second nature to me. If I was on a shoot, I would go home and learn the lines for the next day. By then, I found that pretty straightforward. Compared to rep, it was a breeze.

And there were other, particular things: like learning how to play a drunk, for instance. I was taught in rep that drunks don't act drunk. They try to act as though they're sober and that's when it comes unstuck. But it's an important distinction if you're going for authenticity. I was picking up tips like that all the time. Rep taught me to keep my ears open and my eyes peeled all the time.

You never stop learning your craft?

Yes, it never ends. You become a teacher, as well, of course, and I hope I've passed on what I've learned to younger actors. They certainly ask me for advice and it's always a pleasure to give it. But nobody who is really ambitious ever stops being a student. And why waste the chance to learn? I mean, I had the opportunity to perform opposite absolute legends like Laurence Olivier and Elizabeth Taylor and Jack Nicholson. It's constantly fascinating to see how they work. And you push each other, in a way that has nothing to do with envy or meanness.

On *Sleuth* (1972) with Olivier, there was a lot of friendly rivalry, because we were from different generations and the story was so combative anyway. I remember how he was anxious that he hadn't quite nailed the part – until he put on a false moustache and that made him feel like he was really inhabiting the role. He was a genius.

It must have been intense, in a good way. Did Anthony Shaffer, the scriptwriter, come on set to see how it was shaping up?

Yes, he used to come and see us at work. Actually, everyone was also coming to see how this cockney actor was doing in a face-to-face with Laurence Olivier, you know! And the first thing they wanted to know was, why wasn't I talking cockney? Of course, the part – Milo Tindle, who's the lover of the Olivier character's wife – required a completely different accent. He's the owner of two hair salons, quite middle-class.

But I guess people had their preconceptions, especially back then. Anyway, between takes, Olivier and I would relax together and chat while we watched the tennis on telly. He said from the start to call him 'Larry'. It was all very pleasant.

The director was Joe Mankiewicz, who was something of movie legend. He'd made *All About Eve* and *Guys and Dolls* and *The Philadelphia Story*. And his brother Herman had co-written *Citizen Kane* with Orson Welles. Joe knew exactly how to handle me and Larry, how to get the most out of us. So on set it was the best kind of dramatic jousting.

That's where real energy comes from, and how you improve as an actor. It doesn't stop really, and if it does stop, *you* should stop! Evolution and growth are essential to anything that means a damn. It's fine to fail and mess up. In fact, it's odd if you don't. What is much more worrying is if you find yourself coasting. If you're not constantly renewing, you'd better find a new day job.

Going back to your beginnings in theatre: what led you to the West End?

One important moment was being an understudy in 1959 for Peter O'Toole in a play by Willis Hall, and staged by Lindsay Anderson, called *The Long and the Short and the Tall* about a unit of Brits fighting the Japanese in the jungle in 1942. It was Peter's first big West End play, and he was going places. Later on, I found out that West End theatre had never before staged a play about private soldiers in the British Army – up until then it was always about officers. So it was a breakthrough in all sorts of ways.

What did you learn from that particular experience?

Well, for a start, that timing is all. I remember Peter always said, 'Is there anyone famous in tonight to watch the show?'

One night I looked and I said, 'Er, Peter, don't ask me about who's in – but I'll bring two of them round at the end, a man and a woman.' I said, 'Don't look through the curtains, I just want to surprise you with this one.'

So, I got the two of them at the end of the show, and I took them back to meet Peter. It was Katharine Hepburn and Tennessee Williams. I think he was glad he hadn't known they were watching in advance!

Peter O'Toole came to The Spectator *a few times when I was editor. He was great.*

Oh, he was an amazing man. We became great friends and one night he took me out on the Saturday after the show to get pissed. Which I did, as did he. We woke up the next morning and we had *no idea* where we were. We were both fully clothed lying on top of a double bed.

A young actress came in – I forget her name – and said, 'Oh, you're awake then?'

I said, 'Sorry, what's the time?'

She said, 'It's eleven o'clock in the morning.'

I said, 'Oh bloody hell, we've got to get home then.' Then Peter and I looked at each other. I said, 'Er, sorry, what day is it?'

She said, 'Monday.'

Peter and I both went, 'Monday! We've got to be in the show!'

So, we *ran*. But you know – we made it.

And then O'Toole went off to do Lawrence of Arabia *(1962) with David Lean?*

Yes, exactly. So it was my turn to play Private 'Bammo' Bamforth. I took the show out on tour, along with another great actor, Frank Finlay, and I wound up in a Liverpool theatre – it's funny the things that happen along the way – and we used to eat dinner there every night after the show at this restaurant next door.

One night, I went there and the place was full of girls and I said, 'What's going on?'

And someone said, 'Oh, we've got a group on that's very popular with girls. They've been in Germany and now they're back.'

I said, 'What are they called?'

He said, 'The Beatles.'

So, I met the Beatles very early on! And, later on, I got to know them all well. Especially Paul and John, both of whom I liked enormously – and in Paul's case, still like.

And still your eyes were on the prize of getting into movies?

Yes. I never wavered from that, really. At that stage, I knew I needed to be seen on telly as much as possible. And I did a beer commercial back in 1959 – the jingle was 'What we want is Watneys' to the melody of 'One Man Went to Mow'. I'm a squaddie in his beret, gasping for a pint of Watneys! I think you can still see it online.

At the time, it was still scary being in front of a camera. But it earned me a few bob and, better still, got me the sort of exposure that you can't get in theatre. That's why I did lots of telly, *Dixon of Dock Green*, things like that. Little parts to start with – you know, the copper who comes in at the end when the mystery has been solved to take away the villains.

I remember getting a decent role in a TV play called *The Other Man* (1964) with Siân Phillips – who was married to Peter O'Toole at the time – and a few days after it was broadcast I bumped into my friend Terence Stamp and he said, 'Michael, I saw you, you're going to be a star.'

So I must have been getting something right. In any case, I had no Plan B at the time. I got more creative later in life in thinking of pursuits outside acting, and branching out, but as a young man it was the only thing I wanted to do.

Beyond sheer grit and persistence, how can a person stay focused on a dream or a life goal?

What I would say is that you need to surround yourself with truth-tellers in your working life, or at least have access to a few of them. Even if it's fleeting. One of mine, though we didn't work together long, was Joan Littlewood. She'd been an actual member of the Communist Party, which was odd for me, as I'd been fighting communists in Korea not long before.

Anyway, there I was in doing a stint with her Theatre Workshop company in the East End.

She was known for her very strict approach to acting style, her left-wing politics, and, later on, for *Oh What a Lovely War!* So I was on stage, doing a dress rehearsal, and she said to me, 'What's the *matter* with you, Michael?'

I said, 'Nothing, I thought it was good that bit I just did.'

She said, 'Michael, this is a group theatre and you are an individual, you want to be a star, go to the fucking West End.' And she fired me on the spot.

Now, that might sound like a bad news story. But she was absolutely right. I wasn't cut out for an artsy left-wing theatre company at all. I wanted to be at the heart of things, and she could see that.

Did you know that at the time?

Not really, I was just trying to make a couple of quid. I started work at £5 a week and then I moved to £10, and then I got to the maximum of £15. I just wanted to make a living. I did theatre in order to learn to act. Yes, I wanted to be a movie actor – but not a movie *star*. You don't think of yourself like that, certainly when you're just trying to make ends meet.

But Joan saw immediately that I was a fish out of water in her setting. That's what I mean about truth-tellers. The truth is sometimes hard to hear, but you need people who are honest enough to tell you how things really are. Otherwise you can waste years in blissful ignorance, not realising that you're on completely the wrong track. And everybody has a different track.

Who have been the other truth-tellers in your career?

There have been loads – above all my wife Shakira, of course, whom I trust and listen to more than anyone. She is the kindest and wisest person I've ever met. But, outside my family, another important figure worth mentioning is Dennis Selinger, who became my agent after he saw me in a TV movie written by Johnny Speight called *The Compartment* in 1961. It was like fate, because I had written to him asking him to represent me – and before he got my letter, he had written to me offering to do so. Would you believe, our letters crossed!

As far as work was concerned, Dennis was the best person in my life. He represented Sean Connery, Roger Moore, David Niven and Peter Sellers, too. And he always made time for me. Before I got married, I had dinner with him three times a week. The point about him was that he wanted me to earn money, of course, but he also wanted me to do really good work, too, that would build up my reputation.

So, for instance, he got me to do *Next Time I'll Sing to You* by James Saunders at the New Arts Theatre in London in 1963 – and then transferred to the Criterion in the West End. The pay wasn't great, but the reviews were. And he could see that I would do well in it.

So I had people like Orson Welles coming backstage to congratulate me and Stanley Baker, too – which led to *Zulu* (1964).

Dennis was able to think strategically. And, however sharp you are, you need people like him in your life to help you take wise decisions that will benefit you in the medium and long term, as well as in an immediate sense.

It's no accident that we asked Dennis to be godfather to our daughter Natasha. And we still miss him: he died in 1998. That kind of friend is very special, believe me, and when they come along you should keep them close for as long as you possibly can.

My big break. The cockney actor plays the officer in *Zulu*.

2

The Sixties – And How to Have Your Very Own Magical Moment

You're closely identified with the Sixties and its transform-
ations. How aware were you at the time of how important it all
was?

Well, obviously nobody called it 'the Sixties' to start with. That
came later, when all the bloody sociologists and journalists
climbed on board. And it didn't all happen at once. Looking
back, though, the first moment I felt like the earth might be
shifting a bit was *before* 1960. And it was only a feeling.

There were three of us, all actors, all broke, hanging out in
this café just off Leicester Square in the Arts Theatre – all the
out-of-work actors used to go there to sit and shoot the breeze.
There was me, John Osborne and a guy called David Baron.
John said, 'You know what? I'm working on a play.' And that
turned out to be *Look Back in Anger* (1956).

And then David said, 'Well, I'm working on a play, too. And
I want you to act in it, Michael.'

I said, 'That's fabulous, thank you.' To be honest, people were
always saying stuff like that, meaning well, so I didn't take it
too seriously.

But David went on, 'Also, I'm going to write it under my own name. Harold Pinter.'

What was the play?

It was called *The Room*, and – eventually – I did go on to do it in 1960 at the Royal Court Theatre in London. Harold's wife at the time, Vivien Merchant, also had one of the main parts.

So – going back to your conversation with Pinter and Osborne – you caught the scent of change in the air?

Maybe it's hindsight, but, yes, I think so. Just a bit. Here were three guys who were all doing new stuff, trying new things. Or were about to, anyway. And that was what the whole thing was all about, this thing called the Sixties. It was about ignoring all the old social barriers and all the voices saying, 'People like you *can't do things like this.*'

It was almost an unconscious collective decision by a generation to say: 'No more, it's our turn.'

Right. I mean, nobody held a meeting in 1959 and said, 'This is what we all agree is going to happen, starting next year!' It was much messier than that, and much more fun.

What was your role in it all?

Well, don't forget, I was already twenty-six when the Sixties began. I'd seen and done a fair bit already. Not that much older than everyone else, but just enough to sense that things were getting different and more exciting. But it was all about doing, not analysing. We were too busy to analyse it all.

What sort of things?

For starters, all the exciting people seemed to be in the same place at any one time. Music drove a lot of that. And not just live music, either. The clubs and the discotheques. There was a place called the Ad Lib owned by the art dealer Oscar Lerman, who was American and married to Jackie Collins. They became great friends of ours in Hollywood, we loved them both. Anyway, you'd go up to the Ad Lib and *all* of the Beatles and *all* of the Rolling Stones would be in – on the same night. That would be perfectly normal.

And, you know, none of us were talking about some social movement. We were looking to make a few quid and have a great time. It wasn't self-conscious at all, there was no time to be self-conscious.

So there was no sense of history?

No, you can't set out to make history. And, when you're young, you don't care about that sort of thing. You just want to be there when the exciting stuff happens. And we were. There was all the fashion on the King's Road, with the miniskirts and Mary Quant. Bands popping up all the time, R&B playing everywhere. It was all about possibility.

Restaurants had only been for people in suits, stuffed shirts. And now there were restaurants where people like me could go and have a meal, without having to wear a tie and dress like an accountant or a banker. You'd find like-minded people and gravitate towards them. Like David Bailey, we were like brothers, a pair of cockney boys made good. It was lovely.

The point is, though, that you and other people like you were primed for it – that sense of possibility, I mean.

Correct. People often ask me, 'Could something like the Sixties happen again?' And it's the wrong question. The real question is: are you ready to take advantage of opportunities like that when they pop up out of nowhere? Do you have the skills and the sense of purpose you need to squeeze all the juice out of the lemon? Part of it is being in the right place at the right time, of course. And I was. But you also have to be mentally and professionally ready to step up when someone gives you a chance.

Who gave you your chance?

Well, I've already mentioned Stanley Baker coming to see me in a play. And he must have liked what he saw because he fixed for me to go for an audition for a film he was starring in – which turned out to be *Zulu*. The point is that he and the director, Cy Endfield, were looking for an actor to play a cockney corporal in the story of the battle of Rorke's Drift. And Stanley said, 'Go and see Cy in the bar of the Prince of Wales Theatre tomorrow morning at ten – best of luck.' Well, this was exciting, but I was pretty realistic by then about how many things that looked great actually worked out.

So I went in and – what do you know? – they said, 'Oh, we're so sorry, Michael, we've actually cast someone in the role already, sorry for taking your time.' All very polite.

I just put it down to experience and said, 'That's all right, don't worry.' And I started to make my way out of the theatre.

Only then Cy, the director, called out and said, 'Hang on a minute – how tall are you?'

And I said, 'Oh – I'm six foot two.'

You must have been wondering what this was all about.

Yes, I thought my chances with that movie had already vanished. But Cy went on, 'You know, you don't look like a corporal. You look like an officer. Come back on Friday and we'll do a screen test for you for the part of Lieutenant Gonville

Bromhead.' So, all of a sudden, I'm back in the game. 'Can you do a posh accent?' he asked.

I said, 'I've been in rep for nine years, I can do any accent you want!' And that was how I got cast in *Zulu* and how my movie career began.

How big a part did chance play in that?

One big part. If Cy Endfield had been an English director, it wouldn't have *occurred* to him to give a role like that to a working-class actor. But because he was American that wasn't a factor for him. Which was a real break for me. And, to be honest, my screen test wasn't great, and he told me so. But he saw something in me and gave me the part anyway.

On the other hand, I wouldn't have been at the audition at all if I hadn't already built up a bit of a reputation on stage and I wouldn't have been confident enough to try for the part if I didn't know from all my years in rep that I could nail any accent they asked me to do. As a model for the part, I had in mind a lieutenant from the Queen's Royal Regiment I'd known when I was a private. And Prince Philip, too. I was as ready as I was ever going to be. So a lot of things converged.

The funny thing is, if I had played the corporal, everybody would have forgotten me immediately. What caught people's attention was this cockney actor playing an upper-crust officer. *That* was new.

The readiness is all?

Absolutely. It feels like winning the Lottery, but it wasn't really. The old saying that the harder you work, the luckier you get – there's a lot to be said for that. People look back on the Sixties now as though it all happened magically and it might seem like that now. But actually all these people were really talented and really put the hours in.

The Beatles had perfected their act in Germany. The Rolling Stones were just a regular R&B band for quite a while, learning to play really well and then write great songs of their own. David Bailey didn't become the most famous photographer in the world overnight.

Same with me. There's always a lot of sweat behind the stardust. For *Zulu*, I went off and spent lots of time with officers in the Grenadier Guards to see how they interacted with each other. And then it was off to South Africa.

How did Zulu *change things?*

Oh, completely. It was my first experience of Africa, and it knocked me sideways – the sheer beauty of the place. It took me a while to get used to the set and the challenge of being on location, and my first rushes were terrible. But Cy and Stanley stood by me when people back at Paramount were ready to sack me for making rookie errors. And I justified their faith in the end.

It all came together, especially those epic battle scenes, which I still think stand the test of time, even compared to today's CGI effects in blockbuster movies. It was a big hit at the box office and with the critics. And I got good notices, which was exciting.

The effect on my career was pretty instant. I mean, suddenly I was choosing scripts rather than trudging from one audition to another. And I was getting recognised. The movies could do that for you overnight back then. Not so much now – people stay at home, glued to their screens. But back then going to the pictures was still a ritual of life that brought everyone together at the weekend. And if you were up on the big screen, you were going to be recognised in the street.

And it led pretty much directly to The Ipcress File *(1965)?*

Yes. Success is like a currency. It depends what you do with it. I knew *Zulu* had been a great thing to do, and I was very grateful to Stanley and Cy. But I also knew I wanted to go on and do something a bit different.

What did you have in mind?

It wasn't specific, but I was ready to take a risk or two. And then I got this amazing offer from Harry Saltzman, who was a big-deal Canadian producer, and co-producer of the James Bond films with Cubby Broccoli. My friend Terry Stamp and I were having dinner in the Pickwick Club in Great Newport Street. It was a great hang-out for people like John Barry, who wrote the Bond theme music, and my dear friend, the composer and songwriter Leslie Bricusse, who actually part-owned it for a while.

Anyway, Terry and I were getting ready to leave when Harry sent a note over to our table asking me to come over and have a coffee.

Opportunity knocks again?

Well, as far as I was concerned, I was just out for dinner with a mate! But Harry was with his family and, as it turned out, they'd just been to see *Zulu*. And Harry said that he thought I could be a big star. I thanked him for the compliment. But he hadn't finished what he had to say.

He asked if I had read Len Deighton's book *The Ipcress File*, and, as luck would have it I was halfway through it at the time, and loving it. Harry said he wanted to make a movie of it and asked if I wanted to star in it. So I said, 'Yes, please.' And then he asked if I'd fancy a seven-year contract and I said, 'Yes, please,' again. And then, for the hat-trick, he asked me if I was up for lunch at Les Ambassadeurs the next day. Same answer from me. We shook hands and I went back to my table in a bit of a daze.

I'd only been gone for a few minutes, but my life had completely changed. But that's life. You have to wait for those special minutes – sometimes for years. And when they come – seize them for all they're worth.

And the character was Harry Palmer . . .

Yes. He was a sort of anti-Bond figure, an antidote to all the glamour and action stuff that Sean was doing so well, and then Roger. Actually, Len Deighton hadn't given the character a name, so we called him 'Harry' after Harry Saltzman, and Palmer . . . for some other reason, I'm not sure. The point about Harry Palmer was that he was an ordinary bloke, who you'd see making his own tea and cooking and wearing National Health glasses.

All of which was a pretty big departure for a spy movie, right?

Oh, it was totally new. The idea of a movie hero – or anti-hero – cooking for girls. It was revolutionary! But it was a smart idea, because it enabled audiences to identify with Harry in a way they couldn't with Bond. The Bond stories were pure escapism and fantastic for that. Sean was great, Roger too when his turn came. But the Harry Palmer films were more down-to-earth and kitchen sink. He has to chat up the girls, they don't just swoon and fall into his arms. He's not bullet-proof, he's a regular guy. And that was very much in tune with the spirit of the times.

An ordinary guy making an omelette, cracking two eggs at once.

I'm pretty good in the kitchen, but I could never master the two-egg trick! Len himself did that for the shot, which was a nice little cameo.

Do you think the Harry Palmer films are underrated?

I do, actually. People don't mention them so much now. But they really broke the mould of spy fiction.

John le Carré liked them because he thought they were realistic compared to the Bond movies.

Is that right? Well, he was the master of spy thrillers, wasn't he? Sidney J. Furie directed the first one and then I did *Funeral in Berlin* the year after with Guy Hamilton, who had done *Goldfinger* (1964) with Sean. It was odd being back in Berlin, because I'd been there for my National Service. Of course, it had changed a lot – West Germany was doing quite well by then, with all the reconstruction. But it was very tough, too, because of the Wall and the division of the city between East and West. I mean, people were shot in no-man's-land trying to escape from the communist side. There were guns everywhere.

Yes, people tend to forget that the Sixties were also about the Berlin Wall and the Cuba Crisis and Kim Philby defecting to Moscow – the Cold War was pretty icy during those years.

Yes, you didn't want to dwell on it too much, but it was *there* at the back of your mind all the time. The risk of nuclear war, all that. Berlin really brought it home to me. You might know that Vladimir Putin was working undercover for the KGB in East Germany in the late Eighties? Well, someone told me they had dinner with Putin some years ago and my name and the movie *Funeral in Berlin* came up. And Putin said, 'Tell him I saw the film, and I thought it was very funny.'

Art and life converging again!

Yes, it was odd to think of Putin watching a movie I made back in the Sixties! Even odder now, after all that's happened. But movies do that – sixty years after you've made it, they still have a life and people will come up and say, 'Oh, we loved you in *Funeral in Berlin* or *The Italian Job* or *Alfie*' – or whatever is their favourite. You move on, but the film doesn't.

Is that a burden sometimes?

God, no, it's a blessing. The idea that something I made that long ago might mean something to a twenty-year-old today . . . you never think about it when you're making a movie, but now I see it, I find it humbling and exciting at the same time. None of us gave a second thought to the idea that what we were doing might mean something to future generations. But now that it does, it means a lot to me, too.

It must make a difference that some of the key figures are still around. Paul McCartney is still recording and touring. So are The Who. David Bailey is still at it. Mick Jagger is still dancing on stage like a twenty-year-old. You're writing thrillers. If I'd told you in 1964 that all that would be happening in 2024, you'd have thought I was crazy.

Probably, but we didn't give a damn about 1974 at the time, let alone 2024. That was the point, really. This was our moment and we were going to enjoy every minute of it. People in their twenties don't think about what it might be like to be in their eighties or nineties! And lots of people from back then, my friends, have passed on, and I miss them all very much.

But you're right. It probably does make a difference that kids can still see the Stones, or two of the Beatles, or Roger and Pete doing their thing on stage. We still see Bill Wyman for dinner now and then – he's a few years younger than me, and he's writing books too. The Sixties started out as a revolution and it's become part of our national heritage! Funny old world.

Going back to Harry Palmer – the third in the trilogy was Billion Dollar Brain, *which came out in 1967. It was directed, somewhat unexpectedly, by Ken Russell. What was he like to work with?*

Oh, I got on great with Ken. He was terrific to work with. I know he had this reputation as a wild director, but the shoot wasn't wild at all. I haven't seen the film in years, but it was a good one. Probably the least remembered of the three Harry Palmer movies, though. Filmed in Finland, where it was brass monkey weather. Unbelievably cold.

Do you think Harry Saltzman ever had you in mind for Bond?

No, no. The whole point was to do something different. You can't be Harry Palmer *and* James Bond. I loved watching my friends play Bond – still do – but I wanted to play Harry. It was a real experiment with what you could do with spy movies, and it worked. But after *Billion Dollar Brain* I was ready to do other things. *Alfie* had already come out – this was 1966 – and new doors were opening up.

The story of Alfie *is sort of a parable of the Sixties, isn't it? Sex, fun, class barriers tumbling? The counter-culture?*

It came out at exactly the right time. Actually, it was a stage play first, written by Bill Naughton – and it had been a radio drama before that. This was in 1963. A guy called John Neville played the lead in the West End and Terry Stamp took over on Broadway. But it didn't pan out. Then Lewis Gilbert came on board to direct the movie, and I got the part. This cockney chauffeur driving around London, chasing girls, wondering what his life amounts to apart from bed-hopping.

Why was it such a success?

Well, it was a great team. I had a lot of fun ad-libbing and Lewis was great to work with. We had a confidence and a terrific cast – Millicent Martin, Shelley Winters, Shirley Anne Field. And it's not just a romp. Alfie has his dark moments, his lonely times. So, it was entertainment, but again, entertainment that people could relate to.

The other thing was that, amazingly for a British movie, it got a general release in America. And that was almost unheard of at the time – British films were treated as foreign films in the States and given a limited release, like arthouse movies. So general release propelled the movie to a whole new level and it meant that Americans suddenly knew who the hell I was. A game-changer. I was finally commanding the screen, and there was no turning back.

At least, that's the way I looked at it. It was more important for me than *Zulu* – though one led to another. There was a moment when, I think somebody wrote in *Rolling Stone* magazine, everybody in the world wanted to be Alfie.

And it gave you your first Oscar nomination.

That was incredible, yes. Lewis, Vivien, Bill, and Burt Bacharach and Hal David all got nominated too – Burt and Hal for the famous song. None of us won! Paul Scofield won the Best Actor Oscar for his performance in *A Man for All Seasons*. But Alan Arkin, Steve McQueen and Richard Burton all lost out in my category, too, so I was in good company!

That's a great attitude. But you must have been disappointed

Oh, sure. It's only human to think you might have a chance, especially when you're young. But by this stage I'd actually been round the block just enough to know that there was a lot of politics in these awards and – more important – that there would be other opportunities. At least I hoped there would. I saw *Alfie* as another beginning rather than the height of my ambitions. The traffic lights had definitely turned green.

The harsh reality is that most people who become creatively successful fizzle out quite quickly. They have an imperial phase, if you like, of a couple of albums, or a few movies, or a couple of best-sellers, or one hit TV series. And that's pretty much it. Were you aware of that risk?

Not in any precise way, but I knew that I wanted to carry on, and I was determined to do so. Keep putting one foot in front of the other, take some risks, see what happened. I never wanted to rest on my laurels or get typecast. And I had grown up watching Hollywood movies in which it was absolutely standard for people to get typecast. After *Alfie*, I could have played variations on that part for years, made a fortune, and then ended up imprisoned by it. I was determined to keep trying different stuff.

So you'd advise people to treat success as a challenge?

Absolutely. You should enjoy your successes, of course – otherwise, what's the point? But you should treat it as leverage, too. You've done well. You've bought yourself time to do something different and to test yourself. The next thing might not work – but so what? You'll regret not having tried to extend yourself, I promise you.

Hence, The Magus *(1968) – one of the most obscure movies ever made.*

Yes. I'd really liked Terry Stamp's performance in *The Collector* (1965), which was based on another John Fowles novel, so I was interested in this strange story set on the Greek island of Phraxos, and I wanted to work with Anthony Quinn, who played the mysterious Maurice Conchis. You never really know who he is or what he's up to, and the director, Guy Green, made it as weird as he possibly could. We were filming on Majorca in the baking heat.

The truth is, I don't think any of us had a bloody clue what it was all about – but that was another aspect of the Sixties, especially later on: all the mysticism and psychedelic stuff. The movie didn't do too well and I didn't like it much to start with. But I came to appreciate it later on. Haven't seen it in years.

It's a bit of a cult classic.

Yes, and that's great. I love the idea of someone curious to see that film even now. Can you get it on Netflix or one of the other streamers? I don't even know. But it allowed me to explore an entirely different kind of character. Some actors want to do just one thing, but I like roaming around.

In her book about you, Anne Billson says you're the most versatile screen actor Britain has ever produced.

Does she? That's a lovely compliment. I especially appreciate it because I've always wanted to try lots of genres as an actor. Keep testing myself and surprising people.

Is there a risk in deviating from what the public expects?

Short term, yes. They think, what's Alfie doing talking about philosophy on a bloody Greek island? If you roll the dice and make a real dud, you'll know it and you'll feel anxious, especially when you're starting out. But over a longer period the real risk is *not* to branch out. I was an actor for seventy years, and I made more than 150 films. You can't do that if you're a one-trick pony.

I loved being young in the Sixties, it was an absolute blast, but as the party started to draw to a close, I knew I'd have to find different kinds of role in the decades to come if I wanted to stay relevant and interesting to directors and audiences. I knew that my shelf-life depended on thinking outside the box and approaching offers with an open mind.

We should come back to that. The Italian Job *came out in 1969 and it feels now like a sort of last hurrah for the Sixties. A great caper with Union Jacks, and Minis tearing around, and lovable crooks, and Noël Coward thrown in for good measure . . . a big party of a movie. Did it feel like that at the time?*

The funny thing is that, when you're making a movie, you really can't tell what success it's going to have, how long it will last, how it will be seen – in a few cases, even *if* it will be seen. Some movies have wings and fly, and others are 'straight to video' – although we didn't call it that back then, obviously.

The Italian Job just came together. It was like a bunch of stars aligning in the sky. My friend Troy Kennedy Martin had written *Z-Cars* for television and wanted me to star in it. But by then I was set on doing movies. Then he came up with this script about a British gang stealing a load of gold bullion in Turin. By happy coincidence, I'd been down in Cannes and this great mogul, Charlie Bluhdorn, who had just bought Paramount, said, 'Michael, do you want to do a movie?'

I said, 'Well, Charlie, as it happens . . .' And that was how *The Italian Job* came about.

It's such an iconic movie. Did you sense its potential?

I really had fun making it. Peter Collinson was a great director, and I enjoyed working with him a lot. What makes a good director? They forgive your mistakes, and mostly leave you alone to get on with it. My favourite of all directors, the great John Huston, said that casting is directing. In other words, you cast your actor and stick with them. Charlie Croker was also a really fun character to play. That's often a good sign. And the Minis were obviously terrific – these stylish little cars zooming around, made in Britain. The manufacturers didn't see the point at all and didn't really help. Unlike Fiat, who were great.

So I suppose, yes, there was an energy to it all. But I had no idea that some of the lines would end up on T-shirts or book covers or whatever. I mean, when I said, 'You're only supposed to blow the bloody doors off,' when the whole truck explodes, and 'Hang on a minute lads, I've got a great idea', with the bus teetering on the edge of a cliff and the gold about to slide out – I knew they were funny lines. But did I know they would become legendary? Absolutely not.

You can't predict your legacy?

You can't predict tomorrow! I don't know about legacies at all. It's a silly thing to worry about. The best legacy you can have is to love your family and make sure they're happy. When it comes to work . . . it's lovely to be recognised and to be successful and to do stuff that lasts. But it has to be fulfilling in itself, *while* you're doing it.

If you don't enjoy what you do, you need to think again. And by 'enjoyment' I don't mean ease. I mean that sense where you're absorbed by your work and you give it all you've got because it is satisfying and challenging. Leave nothing on the pitch. That could be plumbing, or being a chef, or programming a computer. Or being an actor. It's not the job itself, it's your relationship to it that makes the difference to your life.

Do you think the Sixties were a one-off? Could there be another decade like it?

The whole point is that there couldn't be another decade *exactly* like it. It represented a bunch of things that have been done now – a sort of social opening-up, a freeing of the imagination after the hard post-war years. But that's been achieved now. The nostalgia is great – I made a documentary all about it called *My Generation* (2017) – which was so enjoyable. I love looking back on it and it's interesting how kids born long after that decade was over are so fascinated by it.

The trap is to try and *recreate* it. That's like reinventing the wheel or electricity or penicillin. It's already been done for you! If you want to do something *like* what we did in the Sixties ... you have to find something completely new. The Eighties were also an important decade – success, a lot of tough choices in society, a lot of glamour, a lot of money sloshing about, everything larger than life. But that moment passed too.

So people can have their own Sixties. But it won't be like your *Sixties?*

Yes! Look, every once in a while, there's a big change in culture and the way we live. You can see it throughout history. It's like a chemical reaction, with sparks flying everywhere. You can't plan it or force it to happen. But when it *does* happen, you can join in and bring your skills and your character to the party. Nothing happens by itself. You have to be persistent and open-minded – which is a rare combination.

Do you think the next big shift will be digital and technological?

Well, maybe. I'm not the right person to ask about that! In fact, from what I see around me, I think that revolution is already happening, in every aspect of our lives, but not in a particularly enriching way. Perhaps the big change will be when we bring it all back to the level of human beings, not just machines.

What do you mean?

If there is one lesson you can transfer directly from the Sixties to today, it is that people have to come together in the same space – I mean *physical* space, not cyberspace – for incredible things to happen. Messaging your friends is fine or having a FaceTime call for your business. That's not my scene, but I can see the point, the convenience.

But I do know that you have to actually gather people in a room to collaborate if you want to change *everything*, which is what happened in the Sixties. It really did. We all knew each other, we were always bumping into each other at this party or restaurant or club. And, for all the talent there is around, I don't see anyone doing anything on that scale right now.

There's a reason that John Lennon sang 'Come Together', you know. And – by the way – John was always my favourite Beatle!

Back to basics as Jack Carter. Any questions?

3

Class Act: How to Beat the Snobs, Defy Labels, and Be Yourself (Plus a Bit of Politics)

We should talk about class. How important has it been in your life?

You can't live in England and not be aware of class – especially when I was growing up. All countries have their hierarchies and so on, but this is a very particular kind of hierarchy. It's a way of trying to limit people, keep them in their place.

What happened when I was in my twenties was that a lot of working-class people decided that they'd just had enough of all that. They'd had enough of being left with the Mickey Mouse stuff, while the upper classes got all the opportunities. So people like me, and Peter O'Toole, and Albert Finney – we were rebelling against the old system.

Hence your reluctance to be typecast.

Right. I wanted to be seen as an actor who was a cockney – not just as a cockney actor. I'm not an angry person, but I certainly had a lot of class anger when I was young. Nobody seemed interested in what I had to offer. Who was this cockney trying to do things above his station?

Mind you, occasionally it worked in my favour, if only by accident. I got turned down for the stage version of *Alfie* – never mind that I *was* actually a cockney, like Alfie – they wanted someone posher. But, as luck would have it, that freed me up to do *The Ipcress File* instead and that led to the movie version of *Alfie*, which was a much bigger deal than the play.

What did that mean in practice? Your determination not to be typecast as a cockney actor?

It meant that I was happy to play Alfie – delighted, actually. And Charlie Croker in *The Italian Job*. But I wanted to play all kinds of parts, not just characters who came from my sort of social background. That seemed to me to be a basic require-ment of good acting, the ability to perform any role. It had been drilled into me by the pressures of rep, and I didn't want to lose that flexibility and potential in my movie career. Apart from anything else, just doing the same thing again and again gets boring.

And look at the roles you won Oscars for.

Exactly. This is jumping forward a bit, but the first was for Elliot in *Hannah and Her Sisters* (1986), which was directed by Woody Allen. Elliot is the husband of Mia Farrow's character.

And he's cheating on her with her sister Lee, played by Barbara Hershey. He's a big-deal financial adviser, very middle class, living in a swanky apartment in Manhattan. He has incredibly rich clients. It was a great role – and had absolutely nothing in common with people from my background.

It's a sort of Chekhov play set in upscale Manhattan, isn't it?

Yes, a chamber piece. The characters are all wrapped up in their own little world. A lot of it was filmed in Mia Farrow's actual apartment. In a funny way, it was down to me that she and Woody got together at all – they had that long relationship and made lots of movies. Shakira and I used to go to Elaine's, which was a great New York restaurant, you always saw interesting and famous people there. We loved going there. And so did Woody Allen, among many others.

Anyway, I knew Mia from way back, she used to come over and say hello back in London when she was only sixteen or seventeen. We were friendly with her. And then in New York one evening, she said to me, 'Do you know Woody Allen?'

I said, 'Yes, as a matter of fact, we do know him. Not very well, but he's often in Elaine's. He always seems to come in around the same time in the evening as we're there.'

So she said, 'Well, if you're ever there and you see Woody Allen at another table, invite me along to dinner.'

And so I did. Which is how they really met.

What was making Hannah and Her Sisters *like?*

I remember one embarrassing moment when I was doing a love scene in bed with Mia – and I look up and there's her ex-husband, André Previn! I thought, bloody hell this is going to be tricky. But it was fine. I loved the script and New York as a setting, and I had a great time trying to figure out playing this guy who has everything but is so restless and unhappy. He's running around the city like a fool in this big coat trying to invent reasons to bump into the Barbara Hershey character. And he gives her a book of e e cummings poems to try to win her over. He's romantic but also pathetic. It was a fantastic role, I loved it – a complicated, middle-aged guy who lives in his head and isn't even slightly heroic.

Mind you, somehow or other, Woody and Mia didn't get on so well. You could see the tensions, even then. But I was obviously focused on the part. I was never close enough to them to know that it was all going to end so horribly. Very sad.

How hopeful were you of winning the Academy Award?

Well, by that time I knew all about how Hollywood worked and I knew that your chances can be wrecked if, for some reason or other, everyone decides that it's the wrong year to give it to an English actor. It really can turn on a dime. So, actually, I didn't go to the ceremony. I had just finished filming *Jaws: The Revenge* (1987) – which is famously the worst *Jaws* movie of the lot – and I decided not to go to the ceremony because, as you probably know, it takes *hours*. But I won!

And your second Oscar was for The Cider House Rules *(1999).*

Yes, playing a doctor called Wilbur Larch who works at an orphanage in Maine. And he's also an abortionist on the quiet. It was set during the Second World War era, and based on a John Irving book, which I loved. He wrote the screenplay, too. It deals with sensitive issues like abortion and race, and it has a great story. At the end of every day, Wilbur says to the orphans, 'Good night, you Princes of Maine, you Kings of New England.'

There was a fantastic cast, too, of all these young actors. Tobey Maguire played Homer, who is sort of a surrogate son to Wilbur. And then there was Charlize Theron, who was great, just starting out, as his love interest – and her boyfriend, who's a soldier, played by Paul Rudd. They all went on to great success and it was a lot of fun to talk to them and hear about their hopes and dreams. I've always enjoyed that side of my career – passing on advice and tips to really talented young people.

What it's like the second time you win? I think, in the whole history of movies, only about forty-five actors have won two or more Oscars. It's not a bad hall of fame to be in.

Yes, it was great to win again. I mean, I was almost forty years into my movie career by then. I had got some criticism for that performance, particularly from some guy in the *Daily Mail* – I can't remember his name – who said that I couldn't do an American accent. Well, thanks very much, I can! There's no one

American accent. The Maine accent is very different to, say, the Californian or the Texan sound. I knew what I was doing.

Was there a whiff of classism in that criticism? The suggestion that, even then, the actor from a cockney background couldn't possibly play an American doctor?

I'm sure there was. I love this country, but there's still a longing in some quarters to pull people down, to keep them in their place. The class system is nowhere near as bad as it was. But it's still there, in a less obvious way. It rears its head from time to time.

How should people deal with that? Or with other attempts to keep them in their place – whether it's race, or gender, or whatever?

It's simple, which is not the same as saying it's easy. You should never turn your back on your background, because it's what formed you at the start and you'll get mixed up if you try and pretend to yourself or to other people. You have to be true to your origins and your identity. Everyone knows how proud I am of where I came from, to this day.

The thing is not to confuse background with limitations. If I've shown one thing, it's that those limitations are there to be ignored, or overcome. Hard work and determination – and a bit of luck – can beat anyone's snobbery. The trick is not to get chippy, but to show the snobs that they're wrong by excelling at what you do.

How would you advise people to avoid imposter syndrome? That feeling that they don't belong in a place, or a job, or a role?

I think the best approach is to remember that everyone feels like that at certain times. I remember Larry Olivier being really thrown by running the National Theatre. He had to take tranquilisers, which must have been difficult. And he was still recovering from that when we did *Sleuth*. Now that's the most famous classical actor of all time, feeling imposter syndrome! There's a lesson for everyone in that.

Class makes people feel smaller than they actually are. If you feel like an imposter, look around and ask whether there's any real reason to think that. People may seem confident and actually be incredibly anxious inside. Don't assume that the person in the room with the loudest voice and the smoothest patter is completely relaxed. The opposite could be true. Just focus on the job in hand and doing it really well. Try not to compare yourself to others.

The person to compare yourself with is *yourself*. Am I making progress? How am I getting on in relation to where I'd like to be? The purpose of snobbery is to make you lose that focus, to put you off balance and to make you feel unworthy of what you're doing. Ignore all that nonsense and stick to your own plan. No human being is born better than another.

I remember when Eddie Marsan did the audiobook for your thriller Deadly Game, *he posted on social media that you'd been an inspiration to a whole generation of working-class actors. People like him and Daniel Mays.*

That's great, because they're both terrific actors, and if what I've done has encouraged people like them then I'm delighted. When I did my memoirs, I had no idea they would motivate youngsters to have a go – but I hear all the time that they did. Well, that's fantastic. And if someone reads these conversations we're having now and thinks, well, maybe I should try the thing I really want to do – that's great, too.

What I've always tried to do is to keep people guessing, to try different things. At the same time, I've never ruled out playing cockneys or tough Londoners. I loved doing those movies, if they were good. I just never limited myself to that kind of role.

On that subject and going back in time a bit – what made you want to do Get Carter *(1971)? That was a return to a hard-hitting working-class part, wasn't it?*

Very much so. I loved the screenplay by Mike Hodges and I knew he'd do a great job directing it. It was very dark indeed, absolutely the opposite of *The Italian Job*, which had been a romp. Jack Carter is a really tough character, a gangland enforcer in London and he goes back to the north-east, which is where his family comes from originally. He wants to know why his brother has died.

It's another film that has really lasted. You see the original poster everywhere. It's a modern classic.

I had no way of knowing it would have this long a life. Somebody told me that it was on at the BFI recently and loads of young people went to see it. You can never predict that sort of thing. But I *did* know we were doing good work. Mike and I were really a partnership, making sure it all came together. We worked on a comedy thriller, too, called *Pulp* (1972) – it's fantastic when you find a director that you can work with again. You're always on the look-out for that sort of working relationship. I had it with John Huston, too. And, later, with Christopher Nolan, of course.

Looking back, *Get Carter* is a movie that sort of says: the big party of the Sixties is over, it's going to get a bit harder now. That wasn't spelled out at the time, of course, but it is very much a movie of its era. Britain was in a tough spot during the Seventies. It was grittier, like a national hangover from the Sixties.

There's a scene in it where you walk into a pub and order a pint of bitter, and then you snap your fingers twice at the barman and say, 'In a thin glass.' And everyone stares at you. It's like the scene in any number of Westerns with the saloon bar, when the dangerous guy from out of town comes in.

Probably stole that from a Western! There's a lot of film noir in *Get Carter,* too. Maybe a bit of *Brighton Rock* (1948), as well.

It makes no compromises as a movie. There's nothing feel-good about it at all. Jack Carter has absolutely no redeeming features. He's avenging his brother *and* his family name. And he doesn't give a toss who gets hurt in the process. Which is compelling, but also asks more of the audience.

It was a departure for me, really. Playing a role that was not even slightly sympathetic. If I'm honest, I was bit nervous about it. It was a gamble. On the other hand, it's fun surprising people. Important, too. I wanted people to be constantly surprised by my range, so I never got pigeon-holed as this or that.

And you're reunited with John Osborne, who plays your enemy, the gangster boss Cyril Kinnear.

He was terrific and he really loved doing it, because he knew some gangsters. He hadn't had a role as an actor for a long time. I rang him up and said, 'Look, I want you to play one of the bad guys.'

He said, 'You want *what?*' But he came round to it immediately.

I think he was amused by the idea of upending the way he was seen, which was still as an 'angry young man'. And that was ridiculous – he was in his forties by then and *Look Back in Anger* was about fifteen years in the past. You can get trapped by your image if you have a success. I think that was one of the reasons John took the part.

And you must have drawn on your own memories of the gangsters around the Elephant and Castle when you were growing up.

Yes, absolutely. I had only observed it, but you could see that they had their own code of honour, where your name and reputation are your main asset and you will use violence to protect them. I obviously wanted nothing to do with that myself. But I had seen it among those on the wrong side of the law. It's not a good way to live and *Get Carter* really did say to people, there's nothing glamorous or admirable about all this.

When you did Shiner *(2000) with John Irvin, you were back filming in the East End. What was that like?*

It's a nice little movie about gangsters and boxing. I played a dodgy fight promoter, it was a fun part. But I was really taken aback by the deprivation and terrible poverty around where we were shooting. I mean, you could tell people weren't eating properly, or enough. It was a shock to the system, because here we were at the turn of the millennium and there were still people living in these awful circumstances. It made me think a lot about how fragile communities are, and also how easy it is for people to ignore the appalling conditions just a few blocks down from them.

I mean, there's serious wealth in the East End nowadays. But also people living on or below the poverty line. They tend to get forgotten in all the back and forth of politics. That's still a real problem – people who get left behind.

Was it the same when you did Harry Brown *(2009)?*

Yes, that was about a Royal Marine veteran on a London council estate who takes the law into his own hands when he can't get anyone to stop the violent gangs from making everyone's lives miserable. It was seen as a vigilante movie, and of course there's a bit of that. But I think it was misinterpreted – what the movie is really saying is that life has become so intolerable in these areas that an old man picks up a gun. That's not something to be celebrated, it's a disaster.

We were filming around the Elephant and Castle and I talked to all these kids between takes. You could see that they were facing a choice in life, whether to knuckle down and try and make something of themselves. Or to go for the easy option of joining a gang, getting into drugs and risking their lives for a nice car or a fancy tracksuit. What they needed was mentoring and a guiding hand. Male role models to show them the way. And that's not something you can buy with public spending.

You can't just throw a bag of money into a council estate and assume that everything will be fine. It's much more complicated than that. You have to convince people – especially young people – that if they put in the graft it will be rewarded. That they're valued and equal to everyone else. It's very hard, but it's more important than ever.

Do you think movies like that raise awareness?

Maybe. But movies aren't about policy or politics. That's the job of politicians and public servants. But, when you think about it, it's also the job of *everyone* – we're all citizens, we should all look out for each other. I worry that the idea of neighbourhood and community has been lost. And it's a two-way street: I also think that people get lazy and give up too easily. Kids shouldn't be encouraged to think of themselves as victims. They should be taught to believe that they can make something of themselves. It's important to be kind to kids, but also to make them realise that self-reliance and responsibility are essential. There are no short cuts.

There's an extent to which everyone's life is a conversation with where they came from, isn't there?

Yes, and, if you have the right attitude, it can help to keep you rooted. I went from south-east London to Hollywood, but I always tried to keep my feet on the ground. Kids who are born into wealth have all sorts of advantages. But one advantage of coming from a working-class background is that you never take anything for granted. And I really don't.

I'm ninety-one, and I still thank God every single day for all the gifts I've been given in life, as a family man, as an actor, as a businessman, as a writer. None of it was automatic.

People ask me what it was like to be knighted in 2000. Well, it was incredible. You don't expect things like that to happen, and when they do, you're incredibly grateful. Privilege comes in many forms, and it's a privilege to be constantly surprised. I'm excited that I'm doing new stuff in my nineties, like writing thrillers. That's very much associated with my class. The work ethic, and the pleasure when things work out.

People talk now about the 'classless society'. What do you think about that?

I think it's ridiculous. It's just a slogan. Do these people look out of the window? Come on. There's still terrible poverty in this country and kids who don't get fed and clothed properly. And we shouldn't accept that. This is one of the richest countries in the world, there's no need for it.

So things have changed – but not in the way that is sometimes claimed?

What happened is this. Before the Sixties, there really was a ruling class, an aristocracy. And we broke their grip. Today, it's different. You have a *political* class, who have lost sight of the idea of service. They talk a good game, but they're really just interested in power and their own careers. Of course, politicians have always gone after power, but they used to do so with a purpose. That's why I liked Margaret Thatcher and why I voted for Tony Blair. They both had a purpose.

You have always described yourself as a Conservative, though.

Yes – I like the old school Conservatives, who believed in responsibility for others, and responsibility for yourself. Patriotism not nationalism. That's me. Blair was conservative enough and a very nice guy, so I felt comfortable voting for him. The problem with real socialism is that it always ends up hurting the people it's meant to help by stopping aspiration and enterprise.

Higher taxes always hurt those who want to get on most. Rich people can move their money about, and they do, especially nowadays. But if you're just an ordinary person trying to set up a small business or work hard to help your family have a better life, higher taxes are going to clobber you. That's when people say, why should I bother to work harder if so much of what I earn is going to go straight to the taxman?

Remember that Beatles song, 'Taxman'? That was something none of us were ready for – how much of what we earned was going to be handed over to the Revenue. Nobody minds paying their fair share, but it can quickly get to the point where you're actually raising less money as a country because the tax rates are so high. The reason we went to Hollywood in 1979 was because the taxes had reached 92 per cent! There's no way anyone gains from that. I'm hoping that this Labour lot don't make that mistake, because it can have terrible consequences.

Most people in the acting profession seem to be left-wing or liberal. Was that ever a problem for you?

You're right – most actors and people in the movie business do tend to be more left-wing than conservative. But it was never a problem for me, I get along with people and I don't judge them by their politics. It's good for people to have different views, I like that. I have liberal views on some things: 'live and let live' is an important principle for me. I don't see why actors necessarily *should* be left-wing, though. It doesn't follow automatically.

What is true is that you can lose touch with people because of the political circles they move in. They get into a tribe and that's that. A good example was Glenda Jackson, who was my co-star in my very last movie *The Great Escaper* (2023). It's the true story of a Royal Navy veteran called Bernie Jordan who slipped out of his retirement home in Hove to make his own way to the commemoration events in Normandy to mark the seventieth anniversary of D-Day.

It was a very special film, directed by Ollie Parker, and William Ivory did a great script. Cameron McCracken at Pathé UK very kindly insisted that the movie should only be made when I could do it. And my dear friend, Johnnie Standing, was in it, too, and was terrific. It's been shown all over the world and been a big hit: the perfect last film for me, really.

Anyway, Bernie's wife, Rene, was played by Glenda Jackson, who very sadly died before the movie was released. She was so good in it, such a great actress. And here's the thing, we'd done a movie together about forty-five years before called *The Romantic Englishwoman* (1975), directed by Joseph Losey, quite an arty film. And, between the two films, we'd barely seen each other – in all that time! Not even dinner. Amazing, when you think about it.

It wasn't because we disliked one another at all, but because of politics. She was very much involved with Labour and became an MP and, I think, a minister. And that was her life, totally absorbing. So it was lovely to be reunited with her on a movie before she passed away. It was a real pleasure to act with her again, I'm so glad we got the chance. And then she died, quite suddenly, before the premiere.

If you were in Number Ten – Prime Minister Michael Caine – what would you do?

I would focus 100 per cent on education. I'd make it easy for working-class kids to get a proper education, so they could go on to do any profession or trade they wanted. Apprenticeships, traineeships, the works. I'd spend all my time removing the barriers that stand in their way and persuading them that they could do anything they set their mind to.

When I was growing up and looking for a job, I was told to piss off so many times. People were always asking – who did I think I was? That was the question. What made me think I could do such and such a thing with my background? If I were prime minister, I'd work night and day to get rid of that. There's nothing more tragic than opportunities missed and talents wasted. There's so much talent just waiting to be spotted and encouraged. And you do need encouragement. But part of that encouragement is saying, 'It's on you, get off your backside and have a go.'

You mentioned patriotism. Do you think people are patriotic anymore?

Not as much. I think young people are suspicious of patriotism. They think it's somehow racist or bigoted. But they're confusing it with nationalism, which is very different. Being proud of your country is a good thing. Being aggressive about it isn't. But we shouldn't throw the baby out with the bathwater. I've worked all over the world and I've loved going to new places, experiencing other places. But – even when we were living in America – England was always home. It's all about belonging and tradition. Not mean-spirited at all. You see one side of it when people support England in the Euros, or in the cricket. We should have more of that.

In the Sixties, did you still expect the monarchy to be around now?

I doubt we gave it much thought. But if you'd asked us, most of us would have probably thought that it would survive. By then, it was already pretty clear that the Queen was doing an incredible job, that she was absolutely right for the challenges she faced. And she had such an extraordinary reign. The outpouring of love and respect when she died was amazing – you could see that she had represented something very special to people. And I think Charles is turning out to be a great King, too. The monarchy isn't anti-democratic, it's one of the ways our democracy has lasted. This stable institution at the heart of everything. We'd be mad to chuck that away. I don't think we will, either.

Does it worry you that politics has become so polarised?

Yes, because all the anger and shouting make people lose sight of what politics should be about. Which is to make life better for everyone. My politics are Conservative precisely because I believe in that, the common good and self-reliance. Fine, other people will disagree, and we can have a good conversation. But it should be a conversation, not a slanging match.

It's odd to say it, but that's quite a radical position nowadays – to urge people to talk to one another in a civil way.

It probably is. But people should spend less time on their phones tearing chunks out of each other on social media and more time talking in a civilised way to one another. There's nothing sadder than seeing a group of people round a table in silence, staring at their phones. They could be talking to each other, but instead they're following some pop star on social media or gossiping online. It's a poor substitute for real communication.

Well, social media, especially X, is like an online pub fight.

It's exactly that. I don't really look at it, I have an account and we tweet out things from time to time. It's useful to get out news or a message. But I don't spend any time on it. It's bad for people's sense of humour, and I really treasure my sense of humour. It's got me through a lot of tough spots.

It's obvious that courtesy is very important to you, too.

Incredibly important. I think manners are essential if you want to be a decent person, and I'm glad I learned them when I was growing up. I think courtesy is in decline nowadays and I regret that. Personally, I don't want to upset or hurt anyone. But I also think that courtesy is one of the foundations of life. It's how we get along with one another day to day, and it's pretty hard to do that if people forget to be courteous.

If people come up to me in a restaurant, or wherever, and they're polite, I'll always try to make time for them, because it's a wonderful thing if something I've been in has meant something to them. It's an opportunity to say 'thank you' to the people who have supported me and followed me all these years. I'm very grateful to all of them.

On the broader question, I'm actually quite optimistic about all this. There's so much doom and gloom around nowadays, and I understand why. There have been tough times – with Covid, with the economy, lots of upheavals. And I think we've taken some wrong turns, definitely. But I'm convinced that most people are essentially decent and want to work things out together rather than argue round the clock online. We'll figure it out. We'll get to a better place. That's my message: don't worry so much, work hard, look after your loved ones – and you'll be fine.

You've always loved conversation, dialogue, storytelling over dinner.

Absolutely. How can people get on with each other if they don't talk to each other and listen to each other – in person, I mean? I want to start a campaign to bring all that back. Get off your phones, everyone!

Super-agent Swifty Lazar was my great mentor and friend in Hollywood.

4

Being There: Lessons of Hollywood Life

How did the move to Hollywood come about?

Well, we'd been very happy in a place called the Mill House in Windsor. It was 200 years old, a beautiful place, with five acres and the river. I started really getting into gardening. We'd been living in my Grosvenor Square flat, but this was our first real home together and it was wonderful. We got married in Las Vegas in 1973, and Natasha arrived in the summer after we had moved into Mill House.

We loved having friends there at the weekend – people like Dennis Selinger, Bryan Forbes and Nanette Newman, Roger and Luisa Moore. I really felt I had everything a person could ask for.

And you were working with terrific people.

I really was. Take a movie like *The Eagle Has Landed* (1976) – Donald Sutherland, Robert Duvall, Donald Pleasence, Anthony Quayle, Jenny Agutter – every one of those was a big name. I played a Nazi, Colonel Steiner, who heads the mission to kidnap Churchill. This was based on a great thriller by Jack Higgins – one of my favourite authors – and directed by John Sturges. Best of all, we were filming only fifteen minutes from Mill House! It wasn't the greatest movie ever made, but it was a lot of fun.

And then you made another famous war movie, A Bridge Too Far *(1977) – from the Cornelius Ryan book about the battle of Arnhem.*

Yes, it was a great era of these ensemble movies – Richard Attenborough directing this amazing cast, with Sean, Elliott Gould, Gene Hackman, Anthony Hopkins, Hardy Kruger, Olivier again, Ryan O'Neal, Robert Redford, Maximilian Schell, Liv Ullmann ... the list just went on and on. A William Goldman screenplay. Everywhere you looked, there were stars in every direction. I don't think a movie like that could be made today. It was epic in every sense of the word.

So you were making mega-movies and living with your family in a lovely home. Why leave that idyllic set-up?

Well, we were talking about tax before. I was in the super-tax bracket, and it was starting to become ridiculous. Some of my fellow actors had already moved to other countries – Sean Connery, Richard Harris, Roger Moore, Richard Burton, and many others. Eventually, my accountants told me that I basically had to scale back my costs drastically or move overseas. I was a family man by this point, so I didn't want to cut back on the lifestyle I'd worked hard to provide for my wife and daughter.

As far as I could work out, the super tax was really meant to be a punishment for success rather than a way of actually raising money. The government just wanted to hear the pips squeak, and that's not a good thing. Nobody gains – you just drive away talented people.

So we decided to move to Los Angeles, which we both knew fairly well. We both had friends there already. We sold the house to Jimmy Page of Led Zeppelin and off we went. It was sad to leave England, but here was a chance to turn a problem into an opportunity.

In what way?

We moved to Hollywood in 1979. You have to bear in mind – I wasn't an actor starting out, going to Hollywood to become a movie star. I was already forty-six by then, I'd been in big movies, people knew who I was. So this was a mid-career decision, really.

Do you think it's a bad idea for young people to head for Hollywood in the hope of making their name?

Well, everyone has their own path to success. This was what worked for me. I moved for financial reasons and to be at the heart of the US film industry for a while. But we were also lucky, because this was really the last golden age of Hollywood, when the world of movies was focused in one place and everyone basically lived in a single glamorous neighbourhood. That's not really true today. The movie industry is dispersed all over the world. So if you're an eighteen-year-old actor with big ambitions and you move to Los Angeles, you won't necessarily find what you're looking for.

I suppose that's one lesson – make sure you're not chasing the dreams of the past. Chase the dreams of the future – *your* future.

In those years, you got to work with a lot of directors. In his memoirs, Oliver Stone raves about working with you on The Hand *(1981) – 'Michael Caine was superb to my mind, subtle, even believable in the climactic fight with the creature.'*

That's very kind of him. Of course, he was a young director in his thirties, and he went on to do *Platoon* and lots of other great movies. *The Hand* was *not* a great movie, though. It's all about this artist who loses his hand, which then takes on a crazy life of its own! But I could tell Oliver had a lot of potential. We used to see him and other directors at Tita Cahn's place for dinner – she was married to Sammy Cahn, the great songwriter. And Oliver always used to say that I did my best acting in *The Hand*. Well, I'm not sure about that! But he was just so in love with moviemaking, you could tell he'd make a classic one day. And he did.

What advice do you have for people once they get to their own version of Hollywood? I mean, when they get to a point in their lives when they might be meeting people all the time who can have a big effect on their success or failure?

I think an easy mistake to make is to think that, once you've had a bit of success, you can sort of carry on without support and guidance. You think that you know all the answers. Trouble is, in any walk of life, whatever it is, the answers are often changing. I mean, look at how the internet has changed everything. You always need the right advice, wise people to act as your sounding boards and your champions.

It takes a village to raise a movie star?

Well, maybe not a whole village but certainly a short street! A very important person for me in this respect was Swifty Lazar – his first name was actually Irving. Only five foot tall, but a power pack of an agent. He'd represented Bogart, which was obviously a massive thing for me. In fact, it was Bogart that gave him the nickname 'Swifty', because he'd got him three movie deals in a single day.

His list of clients also included people like Gene Kelly, Elizabeth Taylor and Cary Grant. And he really made Shakira and me feel at home in Hollywood, introducing us to everyone. He always had my back, working the angles, looking for the next thing. One day, he called me up and said, 'Michael, I've just got you a lot of money to write your autobiography!'

I said, 'Er, thanks very much!' And that was that. Suddenly, I was a writer!

But I loved that about him. He knew I'd enjoy a new challenge, and I did. Really, I've been so lucky in the people who have represented me. The amazing Toni Howard has been my Hollywood agent since 1994 and she has been fantastic over those thirty years – we're great friends with her, too.

How important was Shirley MacLaine at the start of your Hollywood career?

Hugely important. And very generous. We had done *Gambit* (1966) together, and it was down to her that I had got that movie. I played a thief and she was a chorus girl – Herbert Lom was in it too, a very nice suspense comedy. And she threw a wonderful party for me. I couldn't believe the people who turned up – it was like being a kid back in the stalls at the Trocadero! Gloria Swanson, Frank Sinatra, Liza Minnelli. And then Sidney Poitier walked in. It was amazing.

That night was a sort of meet and greet. But some of the people I met at that party went on to become great friends of ours. Like Sidney – I loved Sidney. We saw a lot of one another and we worked together, too. We did *The Wilby Conspiracy* (1975) – that was before I moved to Hollywood, but we spent a lot of time together. It was a good movie, directed by Ralph Nelson, and shot in Kenya. But it was actually about South Africa and the evils of apartheid. I was proud of being a part of that movie, because the message really mattered.

Sidney was invited to meet the Kenyan president, Jomo Kenyatta, in Nairobi, and he always got better food than the rest of us at the hotel! It was terrific to spend all that time with him. He was the kindest man you could hope to meet.

And you played Nelson Mandela and F.W. de Klerk together, didn't you?

Yes, that was much later, in the Nineties. By then apartheid had fallen, so we headed off to Cape Town together to make this TV movie together. I had to work hard on my accent, because I wanted to get it right – it's an odd business playing real people, especially when they're still around. I met de Klerk and talked to him quite a lot, watching him chain-smoke, and Sidney met Mandela, who was very complimentary about everything he had done for the cause of freedom.

How different was Hollywood in the Eighties to the London of the Sixties?

Oh, very different. It was really a small community, focused on the movie business. What it had in common with London in the Sixties was the importance of people getting together – that would be called networking nowadays, I suppose, but for us it was just a lot of fun. We had a house where the pool came into the kitchen! And we were always hosting cookouts for all our friends.

Who would come along?

Oh, loads of people. Somebody told me that there's a documentary about Jackie Collins . . .

Yes – Lady Boss *(2021). It's very good.*

. . . and that there's home movie footage of us at all these parties with Jackie, who was a great friend. Me smoking cigars, which I don't anymore! It was a really happy time in our lives. There were always people dropping in: Leslie and Evie Bricusse, Johnny Gold, who founded Tramp nightclub in London, Anna Murdoch who was married to Rupert Murdoch at the time – they had a place near ours.

Did you miss England?

Yes, and we were pretty sure we'd go back sooner or later. But we wanted to enjoy this time – me, Shakira and Natasha. You never knew what was going to happen next, which movie legend you'd bump into.

Who, for example?

Well, Gregory Peck used to invite us to dinner a lot. And I became great friends with Cary Grant, who was in his seventies by then. A wonderful man. One day, we were at his place having dinner and he said, 'You live over there somewhere, don't you?' It was a couple of hills away.

I said, 'Yes, you see that hill there, it's behind there. The house was built by Barbara Hutton.' And he nodded, so I carried on, 'You won't know this, Cary, but she was an heiress to the Woolworths fortune.'

He smiled and said, 'Michael, I was *married* to her.'

And that was the thing about Hollywood in those days – everything was connected somehow.

Do you think that's true of life generally? The connectedness?

Yes, and I suppose everyone on the planet is connected to everyone else now, aren't they? By the internet. But it's not the same. I'm talking about a much more concentrated community, which I don't think really exists so much now.

Why is that?

I think the world works differently today. So much is done on a computer or phone. And a lot of parties and dinners are corporate now or sponsored. There was some of that back then, but most of it was just people being hospitable. It was less forced.

So this was another cultural moment?

Yes, and this was at the start of the Eighties, when you had a sense of the sun coming out again. Not just literally – though it did where we were living! I mean, in terms of success, and excitement, and things getting moving.

How did you fit into that moment as an actor?

It was an opportunity to do work of all kinds. Opportunities just came up and I wanted to be adventurous.

Like Dressed to Kill *(1980)?*

That's a good example. Brian De Palma was a really interesting director, sort of the Hitchcock of his generation. And I played this transsexual killer, a psychotic character who's completely deranged. Angie Dickinson was in it and Nancy Allen, who was married to Brian at the time. It was very controversial, of course. But the film turned out well.

Quentin Tarantino is a great admirer of that film and your performance in it. It owes a lot to Psycho, *doesn't it?*

Yes, like so many thrillers. The point is: I wanted to be different. I didn't have any prejudices at all, and I felt it was important to stretch myself. In those days, it was considered courageous to play a gay character, let alone a transvestite murderer! Well, I'd already played a homosexual character in *California Suite* (1978) and I did it again in *Deathtrap* (1982), which Sidney Lumet directed. My co-star was Christopher Reeve – a great guy. And he'd been Superman!

So with *Dressed to Kill*, it was just another challenge. I think it's a mistake for actors to think that audiences can't distinguish between them and the characters they play. I'm me, I'm not Alfie, or Jack Carter, or Alfred, the butler. People know this. It's a silly thing to worry about. I mean, the gift of acting is the chance to walk in another person's shoes and to see how far your imagination will carry you.

And the year after Dressed to Kill, *you played a footballer.*

Yes, in *Escape to Victory* (1981). My second film with the great John Huston, a few years after *The Man Who Would Be King* (1975). It's about a bunch of Allied prisoners during the war, who play an exhibition match in 1943 against the Germans. We filmed in Budapest. And the cast was amazing again: Bobby Moore, Pelé, Ossie Ardiles, and Sylvester Stallone in goal! They also brought in a bunch of Ipswich Town players, as I remember.

Sly was great fun, though he was busy working on the latest *Rocky* movie, too, so he had to fly off and do that all the time. I think he used to do writing in his hotel room on that, when he was meant to be learning his lines for our movie. It worked out, though, somehow. And he was committed to this incredible body-building regime so he would be in peak shape when they filmed him boxing in whichever *Rocky* it was. We'd finish a take and he'd start doing push-ups or laps round the pitch. It was exhausting just watching him.

Sly was in the early days of his stardom, and he could have been a nightmare, but as it turned out, he was a good bloke. We had in common our working-class roots – he was the guy from Flatbush, in New York, that everyone had written off until he wrote this little film about boxing and insisted on starring in it. And it won the Oscar for Best Picture. He had that single-minded determination. You need that, whatever you set out to do in life. But what impressed me was how easy-going he was. He was incredibly focused but also wanted to get on with people. It's the right combination, in any career.

This was also one of the last films John directed. He was getting a little bit frail by then, but he was still the master of moviemaking.

I think the very last one he made was The Dead *(1987), based on the James Joyce story.*

That sounds right. There was no one like him, really. I remember Sly was taken aback by how little he intervened, how much he trusted his actors. But that was John. He cast you and then let you get on with that. It's the best kind of leadership – you hire someone, but you don't micromanage. It's a tip for anyone in a position of authority. Recruit the best people and then leave them be. And own your hiring mistakes, if you make them.

With people like John Huston and Gregory Peck and the others, did you feel as though you were watching a great generation doing its last work?

Very much so. It's what happens as you approach middle age – you're conscious that the generation above you is passing on. It can take you aback sometimes. I remember sitting next to Yul Brynner at dinner in the mid-Eighties. And in those days, at the end of the meal, the gentlemen would head off into one room and smoke cigars, and the ladies would sit there and smoke cigarettes and talk together.

So I went with Yul Brynner and poured drinks and lit up. And I noticed that he wasn't smoking. I said, 'Don't you smoke cigars?'

He said, 'No, I have lung cancer, I'll be dead in a month.' So I put my cigar out, as a matter of common courtesy, and he said, 'You go ahead and smoke, Michael, it's not going to save me.'

And he did pass away not long after. Little things like that happened to you and you remember them for the rest of your days.

How well did you know Richard Burton?

Pretty well. I remember going to see him play Hamlet at the Old Vic on my own. It was a famous performance, so years later I mentioned it to him at dinner. I said, 'You were very good, but it was the shortest *Hamlet* ever.'

Richard said, 'Well you have to remember, Michael, pubs shut at half past ten then!'

He could be the most charming man in the world – and then lash out for no reason. I was in a movie with Elizabeth Taylor called *Zee and Co.* (1972), and this was when they were still married, the first time round. When we wrapped, it was Christmas, and, as they were leaving, I said, 'Merry Christmas to both of you.'

Richard turned round and shouted, 'Go fuck yourself, Michael.'

Well, that seemed a little unusual! At the time, I thought he might actually hate me for some unfathomable reason, but,

Humphrey Bogart, seen here in *The Treasure of the Sierra Madre*, was my screen idol.

Off the bill, but on my way as understudy to Peter O'Toole in this famous production.

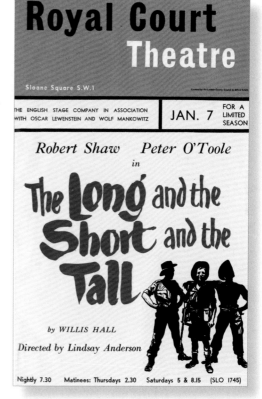

Royal Court
Theatre

Sloane Square S.W.1

THE ENGLISH STAGE COMPANY IN ASSOCIATION
WITH OSCAR LEWENSTEIN AND WOLF MANKOWITZ

JAN. 7

FOR A
LIMITED
SEASON

Robert Shaw   Peter O'Toole
in

The Long and the Short and the Tall

by WILLIS HALL

Directed by Lindsay Anderson

Nightly 7.30   Matinees: Thursdays 2.30   Saturdays 5 & 8.15   (SLO 1745)

'The weird thing is that I get to play you in the remake.' A word in Larry's ear during the making of *Sleuth*.

Wednesday dinners at the Savoy with Noël Coward were an incredible treat.

Cooking with Harry: busy in the kitchen in *The Ipcress File*.

What were the Sixties like? That Alfie grin says it all.

The Italian Job: 'Hang on a minute lads, I've got a great idea.'

My first Oscar-winning performance as Elliot in *Hannah and Her Sisters*, pursuing Lee (Barbara Hershey).

Since I wasn't at the ceremony, Roger and Luisa Moore presented me with the Oscar.

Glenda Jackson and me in *The Romantic Englishwoman* (1975) . . .

. . . and reunited half a century later in *The Great Escaper* (2023).

My most daring role? Brian De Palma's *Dressed to Kill* lived up to its title.

Perhaps my best performance of all, as Frank in Lewis Gilbert's *Educating Rita*.

With Sidney Poitier in *The Wilby Conspiracy*.

'First one to laugh pays for dinner.' A joyous experience making
Dirty Rotten Scoundrels with Steve Martin.

A Bridge Too Far (1977): Gene Hackman, Ryan O'Neal, me, Edward Fox and Dirk Bogarde.

'So explain the offside rule again?' John Huston with Pelé and me, between takes for *Escape to Victory*.

looking back, I can see it was all the drink and cocaine. It made him say things he didn't mean at all. He had terrible mood swings, attacks of jealousy. And he died so young.

He was only fifty-eight, I think. His last performance was one of his best, as O'Brien in Nineteen Eighty-Four *(1984) – opposite John Hurt.*

And he looked as though he was in his seventies by then, didn't he? It's very sad, alcoholism. I saw the effect booze had on him and on Peter O'Toole. It's no wonder I drink so little nowadays.

You must have seen a lot of addiction in the movie business.

Yes, too much. It's not as bad as the pop world, I think. But when people suddenly have a bit of cash and there are hangers-on giving them whatever they want – it's a bad mix. I enjoyed a drink when I was younger, of course, but I knew my limits, and I laid off a lot after the mid-Seventies. It's very important for everyone to watch themselves, especially today with so many drugs so easily available to young people, with God knows what in them.

I don't lecture people. But you need to stay present for yourself and for your family, and if you get lost, ask for help. It's not heroic just to carry on destroying yourself. It's a waste. From what I can tell, there's more help than ever now for people who are struggling and I think that's great.

You had a big success playing the drunken university teacher, Frank Bryant, in Educating Rita *(1983).*

Yes, but you have to be sober to play a drunk on film! That was a great part and got me my third Oscar nomination, after *Alfie* and *Sleuth* – this time, the award went to Robert Duvall, though Cary Grant was kind enough to say that he thought I was the real winner! Anyway, *Educating Rita* was based on a Willy Russell play and it reunited me with Lewis Gilbert, sixteen years after *Alfie*. We filmed it in Dublin, though the story is set in an English city.

I had to put on 30lbs because Frank is meant to be this burnt-out old professor who's just let himself go. I remember watching Emil Jannings as the teacher in that Marlene Dietrich classic, *The Blue Angel* (1930), looking for tips – you can always get inspiration from great movies of the past.

Frank starts teaching this hairdresser, Rita – who ends up calling herself Susan – played by Julie Walters. The producers wanted Dolly Parton, which would have been ridiculous for such an English role. Julie had created the role on the stage, and she was fabulous in the movie. It made her name – she's a Dame now! It's a great story about class, and pretensions, and how people teach each other in different ways.

How important was that film to you?

Well, I turned fifty just before it came out. And I was really glad that I did it, because I wanted to carry on acting and I continued to have this appetite for different parts. You can tell pretty quickly when you read a script if it's going to be interesting or formulaic. This was definitely interesting, terrific writing. I think it's one of my best performances – maybe my best, who knows? – and I am always glad to hear that the movie is still watched by people.

It certainly is. On that point: do you worry that back catalogues of films are going to be harder for people to see now? Now that the streaming services like Netflix and Prime Video have basically replaced DVDs and Blu-rays for most people?

It's an interesting point. Don't forget, there wasn't even VHS until the late Seventies, early Eighties. Only what was on at the cinema, or on the telly. Home video didn't really get going until we were living in Hollywood. So there's been this long period where you could order up just about anything.

I like actually going to the movies – there's going to be a total of four cinemas on the King's Road soon. One of them has a picture of Sean in the window and I can say hello to him every time we drive past! But I see the worry. I hope that it's still possible to see everything, really. It would be a great shame if movies only existed online. I think that would really be the end of movies.

Do you think that's a serious prospect?

Hard to say. I think the business has become much too depend-ent upon franchises and there's less risk-taking than ever. But going to the movies – I mean at the cinema – has to stay a habit for people, not just an occasional outing. There was a time when it would feel odd not to go to the movies at least once a week. I get the feeling that's not true anymore.

I read about cinemas closing all the time and it makes me sad, because you can't appreciate a great movie on the screen of a phone. You just can't. Imagine watching *The Man Who Would Be King* on an iPhone!

Yes, or any movie really. Another great film that has lasted from the period we're talking about is Mona Lisa *(1986).*

Yes, with my dear friend Bob Hoskins. He asked me to do that movie, and of course I said yes. I really miss him. We were both London working-class – he grew up in Finsbury Park. That was directed by Neil Jordan, who's very accomplished. It's a sort of neo-noir mostly set in the streets of London and Bob plays this guy who's just out of jail and acts as a chauffeur to this high-priced call girl played by Cathy Tyson. I'm the gangster boss, Denny Mortwell – he's a really horrible piece of work! I loved acting with Bob, such a talented actor. I think his performance in *The Long Good Friday* (1980) is a high point in the history of British cinema.

Some actors count the number of lines they have in a screenplay before accepting it. I get the feeling you look for quality.

Very much so. *Mona Lisa* is a good example of that. I'm only on screen for a few scenes. But so what? I knew it would be a good film and I wanted to work with the people who were involved, especially Bob. It might sound odd, but if you want to be a film star – or the equivalent in your particular field – you have to be willing to play supporting roles, too. It's not how many minutes you're on screen. It's what you do with those minutes.

There's that chilling moment when you are cutting the Bob Hoskins character, George, down to size: 'I'm good at the little things, the little things that mean everything.'

I'd forgotten that! Yes, Denny is such a bastard, he loves belittling George. And Bob, who was sharp as a tack in real life, was able to capture the look of a man who's intimidated and confused. I loved working with him, he was such a good actor and a terrific guy.

And in 1987 you moved into your new place in Oxfordshire.

Yes, the Rectory Farm House. I had been getting homesick and we started looking in 1984. As soon as we saw it – this amazing seventeenth-century house – Shakira said, 'This is the place!' It needed a lot of work, but it was so beautiful, with a huge garden and two hundred yards of river. It took a while to get it ready, with all the renovations, which always take longer than you think, especially with a listed property. But it was definitely worth it. We'd had our Hollywood adventure and it was time to come home.

But you kept one foot in Hollywood, didn't you?

Well, we used to rent the Bricusses' lovely house on San Ysidro Drive in Beverly Hills, which was a home from home for us. When I made *Noises Off* (1992), we had time to look around to buy another place – which we did. A smaller house in the hills with fantastic views.

That movie was directed by Peter Bogdanovich.

Yes, it was an adaptation of the Michael Frayn play. I liked the idea of working with Peter – he'd directed *The Last Picture Show* (1971), *What's Up, Doc?* (1972) and *Paper Moon* (1973), all modern classics. He was a very interesting man, a former movie critic, but complicated, I think. He was with Cybill Shepherd for a long time, who was really good in *Taxi Driver* (1976).

Noises Off is a stage farce, and I'm not sure how well it translated into a movie. But it was a happy time because Natasha got into Manchester University – the first in my family to go into higher education.

A comedy that definitely worked was Dirty Rotten Scoundrels *(1988).*

That was a few years before *Noises Off* – a dream of a movie. It was actually a remake of a film called *Bedtime Story* (1964), with Marlon Brando and David Niven, about these conmen sponging off middle-aged women. And – surprisingly, given the talent – it had flopped. So they decided to try again, except with me and Steve Martin, and Frank Oz, who had made his name with the Muppets, in the director's chair. He's a very talented director indeed, a real natural.

You can't predict these things in advance, but Steve and I just had a chemistry that really worked. He was this larger than life, off the wall comedian, and I played my part dead straight and we just worked as a duo on screen. It was just one of those partnerships that come together creatively.

Steve and Frank came for lunch at Rectory Farm House before we started shooting, and there must have been about thirty people there. He was a big Hollywood star by then, but a sweet, very shy man in real life. He had been this incredibly surreal, physical stand-up comic, and now he was big in movies. And we had a lot of fun, shooting in all these amazing locations in Antibes, Cannes and Saint-Jean-Cap-Ferrat, places like that.

Shakira and I rented a villa close to Roger and Luisa Moore and the Bricusses, and we had a great time, all of us. Natasha joined us with two of her friends. I've always loved the south of France, though I have to watch it in the sun, as I burn very easily! Making *Dirty Rotten Scoundrels* was one of those times to really treasure and I think it is probably the funniest movie I've ever made.

After the wrap, I said to Steve, 'What movie are you doing next?'

He said, 'Oh, I'm taking the band on tour.'

He had this whole other life as a musician, mainly a ukulele player. Extraordinarily talented man.

How does it feel when you've made a film that good?

Oh, it's fantastic, especially as I got to share the whole thing with my family and my friends. Actually, I took it easy for a little while after *Dirty Rotten Scoundrels*, as I was pretty exhausted. We'd bought an apartment in Chelsea Harbour, and it was nice to take a breather there for a bit. It's very important, if you don't want to burn out, to rest up occasionally. It's one of the secrets of success, I think.

I started thinking about the autobiography that Swifty wanted me to write, and what sort of career I might have as I drew closer to my sixtieth birthday. My father was only fifty-six when he passed away, so I was now in uncharted waters, really. I wasn't necessarily pessimistic but, as always, I didn't take anything for granted. I'd been an actor for more than thirty years by then, more than half my life, and I was thinking about the next steps.

When you're in movies – in any walk of life, I think – you really have to keep the right attitude, which is that midpoint between complacency and panic. Yes, you have to always be thinking, what's next? But you also have to remember: look at the good things that have happened to me so far.

It's not an easy balance to strike, but it's essential. Because any life, any career, has its ups and its downs. The trick is to know them when they come and to understand that each of these moments will pass. That's why I keep a copy of Rudyard Kipling's poem 'If—' framed: 'If you can meet with Triumph and Disaster / And treat those two impostors just the same.'

That's it exactly.

My friendship with Sean was one of the great gifts of my life.

5

The Art of Friendship

You've talked about your friendship with Sidney Poitier, Dennis Selinger, Cary Grant and others. It's obvious that friendship is very important to you.

Incredibly important. And friendship, like everything valuable in life, is something you have to work at – not in the sense of a chore, but taking active steps to keep in touch with people who matter to you. And when you do a job that means you travel a lot, and your friends do too, that involves a bit of organisation! Also, the ability to improvise. Someone calls from the airport and says, 'I'm in town.' Well, come on over!

Is the movie set a good place to make friends?

It often is, yes. I still have dinner with friends that I made pictures with decades ago. But there's a difference between being polite and amiable with everyone on set and becoming true friends. Being friendly and being friends are different. I try to be friendly to everyone, but I don't confuse that with real friendship, which comes about in different ways with different people.

I wouldn't make friends with a terrible actor, either, if that makes sense. I would find that difficult. When it comes to friends from working, we've got to have done good stuff together – that's very important. It's a strong foundation for friendship.

I'd say that if you make two friends when you're working on a movie, that's amazing – usually you might make one, as a rule of thumb. If you're very lucky, you might make three! It's a great thing if you do. Actors are a travelling company, always on the move, and it's great to have people you like and can rely on wherever you go.

Is it a question of trust? Or compatibility of character?

I think friendship happens naturally, when you feel relaxed in a person's company and as time passes you can trust them with your thoughts and ideas and concerns. One tip I'd offer is to be open to friendship and embrace it when it comes along. Another is, you can tell who your real friends are when you are going badly. The people that get in touch when you've had a flop and need a bit of cheering up – they're your real pals.

What's an example of that from your life?

A perfect example is Quincy Jones. I think most people now-adays think of him as the producer of Michael Jackson's *Thriller* and other classic pop albums. But he's also a great composer, including movie soundtracks. And he did the music for *The Italian Job*, which, of course, is a really important part of that movie's atmosphere.

Is that how you met him?

It is. He came on the set at Pinewood one day, and we got chatting, and I could tell immediately he was a great person. I said, 'Look, you must come to my birthday party next Wednesday.'

And he said, 'Hang on, my birthday is next Wednesday, too!' So he said he'd come along to my party.

I said, 'Fabulous. By the way, how old are you, Quincy?'

He said he was thirty-four and I said, 'I'm thirty-four!' Then I thought a bit and said, 'Out of interest, what time were you born?' Quincy said he had no idea, so I said, 'Well, I was born at half past ten in the morning.'

Quincy said, 'I'll ring my mum, she's in Chicago.'

It turned out that he was born at half past ten in the morning too! So we call ourselves 'celestial twins'.

Did you carry on celebrating your birthdays together?

We did. It became a bit of a tradition – not every year, but often enough. For our sixtieth birthdays in 1993, we had a great bash in LA. Ice-T came along and challenged me to rap with him! Then we had another great party for our eightieth in Vegas, with Stevie Wonder singing 'Happy Birthday' and Chaka Khan doing the theme song from *Alfie*. Those are amazing memories, to be cherished.

What is it that makes Quincy so special?

We had a sense of humour in common, and he was such easy company from the get-go. I think that's the heart of friendship, isn't it? You don't have to watch yourself and what you say, you can relax and be natural. When I say we are twins, I do mean that he feels like another brother to me. A great addition to my life, and I hope I have been to his. I can't remember a bad moment in our friendship. And we're ninety-one now!

Another friend on The Italian Job *was Noël Coward, wasn't he?*

Oh, yes. A different generation, of course, but a true gentleman. He played Mr Bridger, the patriotic crime lord who is in prison, and my character, Charlie Croker, has to go and see him to get backing for the heist. Noël and I got on like a house on fire. He used to stay at the Savoy and take me for dinner on Wednesdays. I think he had lifetime privileges there, because he'd done cabaret for them during the war. Something like that.

What I loved about him is that he wasn't just a great raconteur – though he *did* tell amazing stories. I mean, funny beyond belief. But he also wanted to hear the news and the gossip from the younger generation. He loved showbusiness, he was never blasé, and he completely understood that the Sixties represented something new and very important.

That's a real example to be followed in life – to stay curious about what's going on. That's why grandchildren are so fantastic! They are like messengers from the new world around you, whatever it turns out to be. They keep you up to date.

How did you stay in touch with friends when you were all so busy, and working in different places?

You have to seize the opportunity to catch up with people you like. So for my ninetieth birthday, Shakira arranged for Tom Cruise to come to my celebration dinner at the River Café as a wonderful surprise. And I was very touched by that, because he's incredibly busy making big box office movies, and he's so involved in the detail of them all, doing his own stunts and so on. Did you see the stunt he did in one of the *Mission Impossible* movies? Flying off a mountain on a motorbike with a parachute? Absolutely amazing. But he still found the time to come and celebrate with me. That was the act of a true friend.

Have you known him long?

Yes, more than forty years! What happened was that we were doing a big event for *Educating Rita*, and Shakira had left the table for a moment, and I turned around and there was this young actor, very polite, asking lots of questions about how to be successful and not just be a flash in the pan. That was Tom, probably around the time of *Risky Business* (1983), just starting out. I can't remember what I said, but it obviously didn't do him any harm!

Did you know that he would go on to become such a big star?

There was definitely something special about him. He had a great attitude, this sense of poise. What interests me is that he is really one of the last true stars in movies. People will go to see a film just because he's in it. That's incredibly rare nowadays. Brad Pitt is a star, too. Like me, he's kept going through thick and thin. He'll do an incredible movie like *Babylon* (2022), or a Quentin Tarantino film, and then he'll do one that's not so good like *Bullet Train* (2022). But that's okay, he has the star power to move on. I think Morgan Freeman has some of that quality, too. The point is that there are so few in that bracket nowadays – not like John Wayne, or Humphrey Bogart, or Cary Grant. It works very differently now.

Is that because celebrity has replaced fame?

It might be that. When everyone's famous, nobody is!

That's a good way of putting it. Going back to friendship: tell me about the 'Mayfair Orphans'.

Oh, that was something special. And that was a good example of making the effort to stay in touch with people you really click with. It was a group of mates who I'd mostly started hanging out with in the Sixties and we'd stayed friends. And then in the Nineties we started having regular lunches and dinners together – in Mayfair, and because most of us had lost both our parents by then, we were the 'Orphans'.

It was me, Roger Moore, Leslie Bricusse, Dennis Selinger, the directors Bryan Forbes and Michael Winner, the press agent Theo Cowan, Johnny Gold, Oscar Lerman, the photographer Terry O'Neill, the record producer Mickie Most, the tailor Doug Hayward, and the great trichologist Philip Kingsley.

What that gang did was keep alive the spirit of the Sixties as we got older. We were like veterans of a wonderful experience we'd shared and now we all had families and so on, and we were still enjoying each other's company very much. Keepers of the lightning in a bottle.

Like they say: you can make new friends, but you can't make old friends. Not everyone came to every gathering, but we all stayed in touch. It was very life-enhancing and so much fun.

A bit more than a WhatsApp group.

Whatever that is! I think it's very important to make the time, however busy you are, for these special lunches and dinners. I see people staring into their laptops with headphones on and wonder, when do you see your friends? Habits change from generation to generation, but I think human beings always need real contact and relaxation with people they really like. Isolation is not good for people and I think it's easier than ever to fall in that trap.

What's it like to work with someone who's already a friend?

Oh, fantastic. The great example of that for me is Sean Connery. I was only twenty when we met – the late Fifties this was, at a party with two girls on a Saturday night, and there was Sean. He had a great story, which is that they had been doing a stage production of the Rodgers and Hammerstein musical *South Pacific*, with the chorus line of sailors famously singing the song 'There is Nothing Like a Dame'. But they were worried that the performers didn't look macho enough, so they went looking for tough guys – and found Sean, who had been doing body-building in the gym. That was really his start, seven or eight years before he did his first Bond movie, *Dr No* (1962). We became great friends.

And then you did The Man Who Would Be King *together?*

Yes, which was in the mid-Seventies. It was very special, that movie. John Huston directing, one of my best friends playing Danny Dravot, me as his fellow British Army sergeant, Peachy Carnehan, Christopher Plummer as Kipling, Shakira as the great beauty, Roxanne. What more could I ask?

Do you think that it helped that you and Sean knew each other so well?

I do, because it was a very precise film, every detail mattered. It was about two soldiers in India in the nineteenth century, and we had both been in the Services, me in the Army, Sean in the Royal Navy. We both knew the original Kipling story, too.

And John Huston was the perfect director – he let us get on with it. I remember reading that Stanley Kubrick used to make his actors do seventy or more takes. I knew Kubrick well, and I love his movies. But I don't understand that way of film making at all. Often, John would just do one take and say, 'Print it.' He knew what he wanted,

And it was a passion project for him, wasn't it?

It really was, he'd been trying to get it made for years. Originally, with Clark Gable and Humphrey Bogart. And he'd directed

Bogart in *The Maltese Falcon* (1941), *The Treasure of the Sierra Madre* (1948), *The African Queen* (1951) and other movies I loved.

Shakira and I were having a sort of mini-honeymoon at the Hotel George V in Paris, and the phone rang, and this voice said, 'Is that Michael Caine? This is John Huston.' I couldn't believe it. He asked me if I could join him in the bar, and I've never got shaved and dressed so quickly in my life!

So when I sat down with him, he told me about his obsession with the Kipling story, with all its mythology and Freemasonry, and how he'd planned for Bogart to play the part of Peachy. He was finally getting the production going and wondered if the part interested me. I couldn't believe my ears! My favourite director asking me to play a role originally earmarked for my screen idol! Of course, I said yes there and then.

Before I left, I asked him, 'Oh, who have you got in mind for Dravot?'

And John said, 'I want Sean Connery.'

It was almost too good to be true. I remember being very flattered later on when John said I was 'an honest man'. That was one of the greatest compliments anyone has ever paid me.

Did you and Sean both realise the movie was going to be so special?

I think on the shoot itself we were too focused on getting it right to think like that. We were in Morocco on location, imagining these two Army guys trying to find the ancient kingdom of Kafiristan. And they both go through very intense changes during the story, deranged in the case of Dravot. So we were looking out for each other, and also raising each other's game.

I'll tell you what *was* true. Obviously, we both went on to do many more movies. But *The Man Who Would Be King* was the kind of film where, by the end, you thought, if this turns out to be my last movie for whatever reason, we've really done it as well as we possibly could. It's a great feeling, in any career or activity, very rare indeed.

Sean's been gone a few years now, but that partnership we had has been one of the most important things in my life. It's really important to seek out that kind of alliance, whatever you do for a living: that unique form of friendship where you know that your life is better for knowing and working with someone. You have to keep your eyes open, because it doesn't come around every day. If it does – seize the opportunity and you won't regret it.

Were there particular times when friendship helped you?

I'll give you a good example of how it has – and unexpectedly so. I was in a bit of a dip in my career and thinking it might be time to hang up my hat. I was approaching sixty, after all, starting to do other things, and enjoying them. And we were living in Miami and really loving it. Lots of restaurants and clubs had opened. In fact, I opened a restaurant of my own – we'll get to that. It was really booming, with a great nightlife.

Suddenly, it didn't seem necessary to spend quite so much time in LA, as much as we still liked it. In Miami, we found that there was a sort of impromptu group of showbusiness people. Sly Stallone had a place, Oliver Stone did too, Madonna was around – and so was Jack Nicholson.

Jack was obviously a legend of our trade and I knew him pretty well by then. But I hadn't actually worked with him. And, more or less out of the blue, he said, 'Michael, I want you to do a movie with me.' And that turned out to be *Blood and Wine* (1996).

Bob Rafelson directed that, didn't he?

That's right. He'd made *Five Easy Pieces* (1970) with Jack, and some other great movies and the two of them had a real spirit of collaboration. *Blood and Wine* is a sort of neo-noir crime yarn about jewel thieves, and I played a safe cracker called Victor. Jennifer Lopez was in it and Judy Davis. I don't suppose it's one of Bob's greatest pictures, but it was personally import-ant to me because it persuaded me that I might still have some more acting to do. And that was entirely down to Jack. He 'un-retired' me. And, as it turned out, I kept doing movies for almost thirty more years!

Once again – you found yourself in a creative community at the right time in Miami. It's a bit of a pattern, isn't it?

I suppose so. You can't predict it, but you have to be open to it. We had spent a bit of time in Miami when I was making a dud movie called *The Island* (1980). The city was not in great shape then. But by the early Nineties it was transformed, especially South Beach. Even then, we didn't know quite how many creative people were around until we moved there, first renting then in a place of our own. But it turned out be to be a very exciting time. When it comes to culture, cities rise and fall. It's a curious thing.

It's very hard to lose friends. But, of course, it happens. How do you advise people to cope with that loss?

Well, you always miss people when they've passed away. I like to keep facing forward, not to dwell on the past. But I don't forget my friends at all – far from it. And I'm old enough to have lost a fair few of them, of course. But what you do is you honour them by remembering them, and talking about them, and staying in touch with their loved ones. Checking in to see if they're okay.

If you know someone who has lost a spouse or a parent who was a friend of yours – invite them to dinner, make them feel loved and welcomed. We still see Sean's son, Jason Connery, for example. It's the nicest and most natural thing in the world, and it's something you can do as long as you live. You can keep the spirit of a friendship alive by keeping an eye out for someone who your friend cared for.

And you've continued making friends with younger actors, haven't you?

Absolutely. One of the pleasures of getting older is seeing how the next generation turns out, what they do similarly, what they do differently. Unless you're a real grouch, it's a tremendous experience. It's nice to find yourself handing out advice, just as you were given advice by the older generation in your own time.

You don't force it on people, of course. That would make you a bore. But, in a business like mine – probably any business – young, talented people are keen to hear what it used to be like, how it's changed, what's stayed the same.

Experience is its own kind of wisdom and it is something you can pass on. But it goes both ways. You learn a lot from young actors about the changing world, and the way expectations are different or similar to the way things were when I was starting out.

Are there any people you'd single out?

Well, I was very impressed by Jane Horrocks when we did *Little Voice* (1998). She played Laura, who's known as Little Voice or 'LV', this Yorkshire girl who's very shy but is an incredible singer. And I was the manager, Ray. She was so good, you could see how talented she was. Same goes for Ewan McGregor, who was just starting out and played this young telephone engineer called Billy. You could see that there was a nice group of talented young people coming through, and I was very happy to be there with them.

And then there was Joaquin Phoenix on *Quills* (2000), which is about the Marquis de Sade, who was played by Geoffrey Rush. I was the doctor and Joaquin was the priest who oversees the insane asylum where de Sade was being held. He was still in his twenties, very intense and quiet, very polite. You could tell he was going places and I wasn't surprised when he won an Oscar years later. Very talented. A smashing guy.

Same goes for Sandra Bullock, who I worked with on *Miss Congeniality* (2000). She was the FBI agent going undercover at a beauty pageant and I played the beauty pageant coach. It was a lot of fun, and Sandra was so down-to-earth and good at the job. It was kind of an updated screwball comedy and she's a natural comedian, very likeable and smart. Again, no surprises when she won an Oscar a few years later.

How did you become friends with Vin Diesel?

Oh, Vin's special. I love Vin. We first met at a dinner party about thirty years ago. I just instinctively greeted him with a hug and announced to the whole room, 'This is my son!' Sometimes, you sense a connection. I just liked the guy immediately, he has a big heart.

It turned out he was going through some tough times back then, so I think perhaps it made an impression upon him to be embraced and treated with love. Anyway, we've been great friends ever since. We actually made a fantasy movie together called *The Last Witch Hunter* (2015), in which Vin plays an immortal witch hunter named Kaulder and I'm Dolan, a priest who helps him. My grandchildren, Taylor, Allegra and Miles loved that film! Vin really speaks to the younger generation.

He's a real star, and multi-talented. A fine producer who also writes scripts and gets deeply involved in the concept of his movies. Shakira and I are really close to him and his partner Paloma. Whenever they're in town, we have dinner together. Or they come over to our flat for a catch-up.

Vin flies around the place with this travelling company of people – a sort of mobile family and support structure. I think you probably need that in the modern business. It's certainly a change from my time.

You know The Rock, Dwayne Johnson, too, don't you?

Not as well, but he's another really great person. Down-to-earth and warm. I love talking to these guys, hearing what they've been up to all over the world. They carry the torch!

The Blond Knight Rises – at the Palace with Shakira, Natasha and Niki.

6

Interlude: A Few Thoughts on
What It's All About (Really)

You said in an earlier conversation that you'd tell me what it's all about. Let me guess: it's all about family?

Spot on. The most important thing. By far. I am a family man, first and foremost.

Do you think there are hard-and-fast rules about how to have a happy family life?

No, I don't. I'm fairly private about my family relationships, which I think is essential if you're in the public eye. I have an amazing wife, two lovely daughters – Niki from my first marriage and Natasha – and my three wonderful grandchildren. They mean the world to me. But everyone's family is different.

So there are no universal rules?

I don't think so. You can't really reduce it to 'handy tips'! All you can do is say what has worked for you. I knew from my upbringing how important family was – that was very embedded in the cockney spirit. I was brought up in a very close family with a lot of relatives and so I knew loads of people, and I am just completely devoted to the principle of family. It's been a constant in my life.

But I don't think you can tell how it's going to pan out for you at the start of your life. You just have to have an open heart, work hard, and do your best to provide for your family when you have one.

We've talked a fair amount about your connection with young people. What advice do you have for them, and how they handle their relationship with their parents?

I'd just say, love your parents. And if that's hard, give them a piece of your mind. Say to them, 'I've tried to tell you, "I love you" a dozen times now, and you don't listen. And you *should* listen – otherwise I'll stop telling you.'

Don't let it fester. A bit of tough love.

Exactly. Clear the air.

How do you think of your own mother now?

Oh, I really loved my mother, Ellen. She was great. A very wise woman who took great care of me and Stanley. She gave me my first acting lessons when I was very small – she taught me to say, 'Mum's out!' when someone came to collect the rent.

She'd want to know what was going on in the world. In the Sixties, I remember she said to me one day, 'I've been reading in the papers about this thing called a miniskirt, what's all that about?'

I said, 'Yes, Ma, the skirts are very short now with the girls.'

And she said, 'Well, I've never seen any in Streatham!'

I said, 'No, you wouldn't see them in Streatham, Ma, where you'll see them is in the King's Road and on Saturday I'm taking you to lunch there.'

So one Saturday we went to lunch, to a really fashionable restaurant in Chelsea. But before we ate, we went for a walk, and within twenty seconds, there was a girl in a miniskirt and I said, 'Look out, here's one coming, have a look when she goes by.' So my mum looked this girl up and down as she went by.

I said, 'Well, what do you think, Mum?'

She thought about it and said, 'Hmmm. Well, if it's not for sale, you shouldn't put it in the window.'

And that was my mum! She said things like that all the time.

What about your dad?

He was also called Maurice. He was my hero, even if I was determined not to follow him into Billingsgate as a porter. He was a brilliant man, who in a different time could have done anything. I get my toughness from him. And when opportunities came along for me that hadn't been available to him – well, all the more reason to seize it. You can completely respect what your parents did, but do something different yourself.

Do you worry about your grandchildren's future?

No, I know they'll do amazing things. They're a great generation, full of spirit and excitement. Their lot will shape this century in ways we can't imagine now.

What dating advice do you have for youngsters?

I'm the wrong person to ask because I am the luckiest man on earth! I married absolutely the perfect person. I knew immediately that Shakira was the one for me.

I finally persuaded her to go out on a date with me, and we've been together ever since. I've always hated being apart from her, I can't imagine life without Shakira. Here's the best way of putting it – I didn't mind being on my own until I was married to Shakira and then I didn't like being on my own at all. We are very different from each other, but when we're together we're one person. And we've been married for fifty-one years.

It's such an amazing love story. Do your grandchildren ask you for tips on love and life?

Taylor asks me how you should flirt with girls! He's old enough now. I always say that patience is very important if you really like someone. It can take a while to figure out if they're right for you and vice versa. You have to give things a chance. You have to pay attention to girls in a courteous way that shows you are a gentleman. I think it's a good sign that he asks.

Mind you, everyone seems to use dating apps now, and I think that's a wrong turn. You can't turn love into a computer program, it just doesn't work like that. Human beings are too complicated to be reduced to ticks in a box on a screen, I think.

Anyway, *that*'s what it's all about.

Last Orders with Bob Hoskins, one of the greatest British movie actors.

7

Staying the Course: Tough Times and the Art of Stamina

I think people will want to know about adversity and how to deal with it. How have you got through difficult times?

You can't always see it coming, that's the first thing to say. When I was in rep at Horsham doing *Wuthering Heights*, I collapsed on stage and I was really ill. Turned out it was cerebral malaria, which is always serious and was even more serious back then. I'd picked it up in Korea. When I came out of hospital, I'd lost about forty pounds. It was really frightening, not least for my mum. Then they found an experimental treatment and, as luck would have it, it worked.

How did that make you feel – just when you were starting out?

The first feeling is real terror, obviously. Then, when I was discharged from hospital initially, I thought my acting career might be over before it had really started. You know, maybe that was that. But I hung on in there and it worked out okay. I got better.

You have to be ready for these things to happen. But don't assume the worst. Life presents lots of problems, but there are sometimes more solutions than you expect. It was a hairy six weeks, but I got through it.

I think people sometimes assume that movie stars glide to success. But it isn't like that, is it?

Oh God, no. I often joke that it took me eleven years to be an overnight success. And it's funny because it's true. I had failure after failure. Until *Zulu*, I was still being rejected all the time. After *Zulu*, I got *The Ipcress File*, and I was suddenly getting scripts sent to me, and a whole range of options.

How did you deal with rejection?

Nobody likes it, that's natural. I put up with it by staying as focused as I could on the next thing. All right, this hasn't worked out. What's next? What you have to decide is: how badly do you want to achieve your goals?

I really did want to make it as an actor and I think, looking back, I had a kind of resilience from my background. My family and the community I grew up in. There was no safety net, really, no Plan B. Life was what you made of it – no more, no less. I was determined, and however bad it got, however often I got pushed back, I didn't break into millions of pieces.

There's a modern word for that quality – 'anti-fragile'.

Yes, that's a good way of putting it. You have to push through failure and understand that there will be other opportunities. And they won't always arise in an obvious way. One minute, nobody's interested, the next there's at least a chance. The question is: do you have the patience to wait for those opportunities, and to keep going through the hard yards? Nobody else can answer that question for you.

If a part didn't work out, I just went to another audition, whatever it was for. I knew there would be something – even if that something was smaller for the time being. I got turned down for some really rubbish roles! But you can't be disheartened by every setback or failure. If someone said, 'Sorry, you haven't got the part,' I just said to myself, well, I don't give a toss.

Did you ever consider giving up?

No. And I do think people give up too easily nowadays.

Do you think they expect instant gratification?

A bit – and to be fair, everything around them is telling them that you can have whatever you want immediately. Our whole culture now is based on that idea. But it's really not true at all. Things worth having and doing take time and persistence.

Life isn't like ordering something online that arrives the same day.

No, exactly. Everything in the media nowadays gives you the impression that it is, but it's an illusion and an unhealthy one. Wanting something isn't the same as getting it. And the two things get confused a lot now. Talent and success can't be ordered up by computer.

I remember you saying once that your greatest asset was your mind. What do you mean by that?

You have to think very hard about what you do and cut through all the nonsense and the noise. You have to make your mind your compass in life and listen to the right people.

I think it's possible to get too hung up on trivia. It's really important in life to work out what really matters. Family, friends, work, fun. It's not that complicated, when you think about it. But it requires a bit of discipline in your thinking.

So persist, but only with the things that count?

Yes, and don't be too fussy too early on. Your future won't be delivered like room service. It just doesn't work like that. From the outside, stardom looks a certain way, but it's the shiny end of a lot of rejection and a lot of sweat. All those people on the red carpet – they've been through more than you'd necessarily think from all the glamour and the smiles and the cameras.

Don't forget, I didn't have any money to start with, so I had to take any job that was offered. If I couldn't act for the time being, I'd take any work that would give me a couple of quid – so if Christmas was coming, I could buy someone a present. It was that simple, really.

And I never wanted to go backwards. Once I was in the movies, I was determined not to go back to rep. I was going to keep going forward.

Were you comparing yourself to other people?

Absolutely not, and I think that's part of the secret of success. Jealousy is a terrible motive – it eats away at people and exhausts them. If you start by saying, 'Oh, I can beat *him* as an actor,' you're going to tie yourself in knots. Of course, whenever I was nominated for an award, I wanted to win. But the reason for that was that I wanted to prove to myself that I'd reached a certain level – not that I wanted to beat all the other people, who were usually actors I admired very much. Acting isn't the same as sport. And if it *is* a sport, it's definitely a marathon not a sprint.

I just set out to become the most successful actor I could become, it had nothing to do with anybody else, and that's why I stayed with it, and *how* I stayed with it. You compete with yourself, you're always trying to get better in comparison to your past performances. And by competing with yourself, you become a better judge of how you're doing.

You know when you have made a disaster of it, yes. Which I did a few times! But you soon realise that it's all part of the process. Because when you get it wrong, you look at it honestly, see what made it wrong – and then you do it right the next time.

That's why *The Great Escaper* was perfect as a last movie for me. I knew I'd given a good performance. It was a success, critically and at the box office, I'd worked with fantastic people on it. You can't ask for more, really. But it was all about the way I perceived it, in the end, rather than how it compared to performances by other actors.

Is that what you tell people starting out?

If they ask for my advice – absolutely. There are always going to be actors who are better than you, and actors who are worse than you. So take no notice of them whatsoever. The trick is not to be the best actor, because that's totally subjective, but the best actor you can possibly become. And I think that rule applies to everything, really.

How did you get into the restaurant business?

Well, this is all part of the same thing, really. Once you're established in your career, you get to the point where you want to try other things, too. You look for a bit of diversity. It's not a question of giving up. It's thinking about how you can branch out, see if you enjoy other things and whether you're good at them.

It's especially good in an acting career, because you go through phases, ups and downs, and if there's a lull, it's great to have something else to focus on. A lot of fun, too.

I'd always liked food and cooking, and I was fascinated by the whole question of why some restaurants worked and others didn't. I was interested in the whole business.

How did Langan's Brasserie in Mayfair come about?

What happened was that Sidney Poitier and his wife Joanna used to take Shakira and me out to this restaurant in London called Odin's. It was owned by an Irish guy called Peter Langan, and one night he came over and Sidney introduced us. He was a bit the worse for wear, but he said he'd be interested in a partnership if I wanted to go into the business.

When he was off the booze, he was terrific. He found this great premises in Stratton Street off Piccadilly and we opened the place in 1976.

It was a great success. What made you think that it would work?

The definition of a successful business is offering something that nobody else has, but that people want – even if they don't know it yet! There were loads of restaurants in the West End, but Langan's had a style all of its own, with great bistro food. We relied a lot on word of mouth and pretty soon there were people queuing on the pavement to get a table. David Hockney did the menu. There was nowhere like it. That was the point.

I used to bring actors there a lot. There were always famous people in. And we had great Fourth of July parties there. I took Frank Sinatra along once, and it blew people away.

How many restaurants did you own?

At one stage, I was involved in seven, which is really a full-time job in itself. There was the South Beach Brasserie, which I opened with the restaurateur Ray Schnitzer on Lincoln Road in Miami – that was very special. Also, the Canteen in Chelsea Harbour, which opened in 1993. Marco Pierre White was the chef and the sous-chef was Gordon Ramsay, which gives you an idea of its quality.

What made you sell up in the end?

I think I'd had my time as a restaurateur. I loved it, but it could be all-consuming. Peter died after a terrible accident when he was drunk. And Richard Shepherd, my partner in the Langan's Group, offered to buy me out. I had a wonderful experience doing it, and I don't regret a minute of it. But, as it turned out,

I was still a movie actor and I focused on that again. And most restaurants have a life.

We talked about Elaine's in New York – that closed down more than ten years ago, I think. Very few places last that long. Or they become boring franchises with branches everywhere, which is a completely different business and much less interesting.

So that's a tip for budding entrepreneurs?

Yes. Knowing when to get out is as important as knowing when to get in. Obviously, you want to make some money from your investment. But if it starts to be a drag, and it's stopping you from doing other things – call it a day. I got a lot of freedom back when I stepped out of the restaurant business.

What about writing?

Yes, I love that. After Swifty got me to write my autobiography, I realised that I really enjoyed that way of spending the day. I did a book on acting, which seemed to go down well, too. And then more volumes of memoirs.

It has always been something I enjoyed doing. One thing about writing – you decide your own hours. There's no call sheet saying that you'll be picked up at 5.30 in the morning! You can start and finish when you like. That's quite appealing when you're used to the rigorous timetable of a movie set.

How did your first thriller, Deadly Game, *come about?*

Well, I'd been thinking of doing some fiction in the 1990s. That was when I thought I might be retired – but Jack Nicholson had other ideas!

Then, years later, the pandemic came along. By then we were living in a lovely house near Leatherhead in Surrey and it was lockdown. Like everyone, I was looking for ways to fill the time constructively. I didn't want to sit around twiddling my thumbs.

I started dreaming up an idea about a copper called Harry Taylor and some missing nuclear ore – the bit in the book about the uranium found on a rubbish dump actually came from a real news story I'd read ages ago in the *Daily Mirror*. That was the original spark, I suppose. And I added in gangsters, and Russian oligarchs, and action in the Caribbean. Before I knew it, I had filled hundreds of pages of notes.

I remember Shakira was surprised when I told her, but it worked out well. That was my first draft of *Deadly Game*, which came out in 2023. That was a great year. I did my last movie and published my first novel! It was something I'd wanted to do for a long time. Shows you can still be doing new things, aged ninety.

So you love being busy?

I do. I'd like to write more thrillers. I love relaxing with my family, of course. But I have a strong work ethic, from my upbringing. You never lose it. And it helps you deal with times when your main career goes quiet. Restaurants and writing have meant that I've always been busy, even between movies. I think having a sense of purpose is key to everything. Drifting isn't good for people. You need to get up and get on with it.

Did you ever want to direct movies?

No. I had one or two offers over the years, but it never held any appeal. I know actors who have gone on to direct. My friend Gary Oldman made a film called *Nil by Mouth* set in Deptford, in south-east London, with Ray Winstone. Frank Oz has been an actor and director. And John Huston acted in a few movies.

But directing is a completely different trade to acting. One doesn't follow from the other. When you act in a movie, you do the shoot and then the publicity when it comes out. And that's it. The director will be involved for much, much longer – often for years. I always think about how long it took John to get *The Man Who Would Be King* off the ground. And he was the greatest director!

What was the worst acting experience you had?

I think the worst was the attempt to reboot the Harry Palmer movies in the 1990s with a couple of new ones – *Bullet to Beijing* (1995) and *Midnight in St Petersburg* (1996). They were filmed pretty much back to back, movies for television.

I could tell fairly quickly that it was a mistake, that we should have left the character alone. I didn't enjoy it at all. But there you go – you make an error, put the cheque in the bank, and move on. And I did.

What do you think about reboots and remakes? There seem to be so many of them now.

Too many, I think. It shows a lack of imagination. Sticking with the same stories, over and over.

I *did* enjoy the remake of *Sleuth* (2007), which Kenneth Branagh directed. This time round, I played the Olivier role and Jude Law took over from me. But the story was completely reimagined, and Harold Pinter wrote the screenplay, one of the last things he did before he died. And so it was a totally fresh take, an original movie in its own right.

Just as The Magnificent Seven *(1960) is a fantastic reimagining in the Western genre of* Seven Samurai *(1954).*

Right. It brings something new and fresh. And Jude is one of that next generation of British actors that I really love. I still think of them as 'the boys' – though Jude must be in his late forties or early fifties by now!

Do remakes damage people's perception of the original movies?

No, I don't think so. The originals are great movies, they can cope with the homage even if it is a bit hit and miss.

I really like Sly Stallone, so I didn't mind doing a cameo in the remake of *Get Carter* (2000). He played Jack Carter, and the story was relocated to Las Vegas and Seattle. I was the loan shark, Cliff Brumby – a part played by the *Coronation Street* actor Bryan Mosley in the original Mike Hodges version. This one didn't really work and flopped at the box office. But Sly had been really keen to do it, so I was happy to help as best I could.

It's funny. When I think about it, there have been so many remakes of things I've done. Jude did an update of *Alfie* (2004), set in Manhattan this time.

And, unbelievably, Mark Wahlberg in The Italian Job *(2003).*

Yes, I can't even recall if I saw that. I know they had my friend Donald Sutherland take over the Noël Coward role, and Charlize Theron was in it, too, I think.

One remake that really puzzled me was the television version of *The Ipcress File* (2022), with Joe Cole as Harry Palmer. He's a talented young actor, but he just seemed to be impersonating me with the glasses and everything, which is an odd way to remake a famous movie. Not my cup of tea. I didn't see the point of it.

There are often rumours of a *Zulu* remake, too. Now that *would* be a mistake!

You always seemed to be on the look-out for new and interesting work. Like Last Orders *(2001), for instance – based on the Graham Swift book.*

Yes, the Booker Prize winner. That was a low-budget British movie and I wanted to do it for two reasons. First, Fred Schepisi was the director, and he's excellent. And second, the cast was incredible. Bob Hoskins again, Helen Mirren, Tom Courtenay, David Hemmings, and Ray Winstone as my son. I played Jack Dodds, who's a butcher in south London, and he dies. The movie is about his friends gathering in Margate to scatter his ashes. It's a little gem of a film, I was really glad to be involved.

Another movie of yours with a great cast was Youth *(2015), which Paolo Sorrentino directed.*

Yes, that reunited me with Jane Fonda: we'd worked together with Otto Preminger on *Hurry Sundown* (1967). In *Youth*, I played a retired composer and Harvey Keitel played my best friend, who's a movie director working on a screenplay. It's set in a resort in the Swiss Alps and there are lots of weird flash-backs. Harvey was fantastic, a total pleasure to work with, and there was also Paul Dano and Rachel Weisz, both of whom are very talented.

I was fascinated on that movie by Paolo's use of digital technology, because it enabled him to do these long takes without worrying about film running out. It was a learning experience – basically a completely new way of making movies. And they got in an Italian composer to teach me how to conduct!

Does the new technology bother you? Some actors and directors are very strongly against the replacement of film by digital media.

I hope that we can have both. There's no doubt that film has a special quality. But I'm in favour of new techniques that enable talented people to make movies in different ways. That's got to be good. I don't see why it should be an either–or. You hear about kids making movies on their iPhones! Well, good luck to them.

Have you had any scary moments as an actor?

Well, there was one experience that was scarier in retrospect than at the time. I was shooting the interiors for *The Quiet American* in Sydney. And one of the make-up people told me, from her experience, that I had skin cancer. Of course, I made an appointment with a top cancer specialist. But I also realised that I couldn't have an operation until we'd wrapped.

So I just put it out of my mind and concentrated on finishing this great part. Which was strange, I suppose. But, then again, work is a good way of distracting yourself. Sydney was also a lovely place to be, which helped. And then we finished the movie and I went back to the surgeon. He said it would be fine and told me it was something called basal cell carcinoma. The surgery wasn't too bad at all, though I did need fourteen stitches.

Looking back, I suppose I could have been more worried by the whole thing, but I was so absorbed by the movie and getting the part of Thomas Fowler right. I picked up another Oscar nomination for that, so my focus was rewarded. I just didn't talk about the cancer, really, and nobody guessed. So my memories of that time in Australia are very happy! Which might sound strange, but reflects how great a time we had. In spite of the cancer.

I suppose there's a balance to be struck between staying healthy and not being paralysed by worry.

Yes. You need to take care of yourself and get checked up regularly. Get exercise and eat well. Gardening was always a great outdoor activity for me. But you also have to be able to compartmentalise a bit, especially when you're in the middle of something that matters to you. I trusted the medical advice then, and I still do. I knew I'd be all right because the doctor had reassured us, and that was good enough for me. That enabled me to finish the film.

It's important, whatever the issue, to look for expertise so you can focus on what *you* do. People spend far too long trying to be amateur doctors on the internet. Trust the experts. You don't have to control every aspect of your life. But you *do* have to control who controls it! That's the art of delegation and trusting the right people.

Is stamina a talent or a skill?

A bit of both, I think. You need to have the ability to keep going in your character to start with. But it's something you can build up, too – a mental strength, I suppose. You have to work on it, like building up a muscle or getting fit.

So it's a question of attitude?

You have to look at everything in the round. I'll give you an example. I made a terrible movie called *The Swarm* (1978). It was made by Irwin Allen, who'd had great success with *The Poseidon Adventure* (1972) and *The Towering Inferno* (1974). This was when disaster movies were very popular – everyone seemed to be doing them. So I signed up as the lead in this movie with bees.

And that was the problem. Bees. Millions of them, bloody everywhere. And not all of them, we soon discovered, had had their stings removed. I spent half the shoot taking cover with the rest of the cast!

I remember seeing that movie when I was about ten.

Look, nobody over the age of ten should be *allowed* to see *The Swarm*. It's a terrible film, and I hated working with the bees. Awful. But then again, I got to work with Henry Fonda. So even that was a good thing to do. All depends on how you look at it!

You've joked about Jaws: The Revenge. *Does the same lesson apply?*

Yes, but in a different way. Two, in fact. When people said to me, 'That was the worst film I've ever seen!', I'd say, 'Probably, but it paid for a beautiful house for my mother, so what's your problem?' Second, I won my first Oscar just after filming *Jaws*. Talk about a contrast.

Shakira and Natasha phoned me from one of Swifty Lazar's parties and said, 'You won!' So I'd just made this bad film, sure. But I'd been able to provide Ma with the lovely place that she so deserved, and I'd finally won an Academy Award, the highest accolade in movies. I'd say that's a bit of a result!

The lesson being: don't agonise over the things don't work out?

Not just that – make an effort to look for the bright side. It's almost always there, somehow or other. Very few failures are definitive or even important. If you make 150 movies, there are going to be some duds. But, really, so what? What matters is that you keep on going. You keep on learning and enjoying yourself. You might end up surprising yourself, you know.

What the butler saw. As Alfred with the magnificent
Christian Bale as Bruce Wayne.

8

It Was the Butler: Lessons of the Christopher Nolan Years

Did you know Christopher Nolan before you worked with him?

Not well. I had seen *Memento* (2000), which plays with time like a lot of Chris's movies, and is a taste of all the mind-bending plot devices and visual effects that were to become his trademark. I loved it. It showed incredible promise.

I also really liked *Insomnia* (2002), which stars Al Pacino as an LA detective who is sent up to Alaska on a case and can't sleep because of the endless daylight. He's duelling with Robin Williams as the killer, and you could cut the tension with a knife. It's actually a remake of a Norwegian thriller, I think, but it's a magnificent movie in its own right.

But I didn't know Chris properly, apart from seeing him at the occasional event or party. I was just aware that he was this brilliant young British director, who was really creative and imaginative. At that point, I was just an admirer of his work.

So how did your collaboration come about?

Pretty much out of the blue! I had been doing a few movies that didn't really excite me – *The Actors*, *Secondhand Lions*, *The Statement* (all 2003), *Around the Bend* (2004). None of them was especially memorable. I wondered if that was that, I suppose.

Then, everything changed – pretty much in the space of an afternoon. I was at home in Surrey one Sunday and the phone rang. It was Chris. He introduced himself and explained that he was going to do a series of Batman movies for Warner Brothers. I asked him what part he had in mind for me and he said, 'The butler.'

I said, 'Hold on, you want me to say, "Dinner is served"?'

And he said, 'Oh, no, this is Alfred, Bruce Wayne's guardian and father figure. He's a crucial character.'

To be honest, I'm not a huge fan of superhero franchises, but I knew that his take was bound to be interesting. And Batman *is* a terrific character. So I asked him to send me the script. 'No, no,' he said. 'I'll come over.'

Turned out that he lived quite close to us. So about an hour later he turned up on the doorstep. He was a charming guy, obviously very bright indeed and full of ideas. No side to him at all. He didn't bring the whole script, only my lines in the movie. That's how he works. I said I was intrigued and that I'd read them and get back to him.

'No,' he said. 'I want you to read now. I can wait.'

Looking back, I can see that it was a clue to what makes him such a good director. He's always polite, but he knows what he's after! Chris sat in the kitchen with Shakira and chatted with her, drinking lots of tea while our Sunday roast was in the oven.

Meanwhile, I settled down with Alfred's lines from what became *Batman Begins* (2005) and, really, I could tell almost immediately that it was brilliant. Just a fantastic new approach to a familiar story. I knew that I wanted to do it there and then. So I went back in to the kitchen, told Chris I thought it was great, and we shook on it. Just like that. It was a terrific moment, I had a really good feeling.

Before he left, he asked for the pages back – everything was very confidential and it remained so. Fine by me. I was thrilled to be involved.

Did you have any sense that you were going to go on and make so many movies together?

Not directly, no. But I could tell that this was an important opportunity and that I was going to love working with him as a director. It might sound odd, because I had passed my seventieth birthday by then, and had two Oscars to my name – but it felt like a big break! You can never have too many of them in life. You can never have too many fresh starts.

Do you think that's true of every walk of life?

Yes, especially now that lots of careers are becoming less secure, but people are also living longer. There was a time when people were set off in a trade or a profession, and then, many years later, retired from the same line of work aged sixty.

Acting has never been like that, of course, but I get the impression that *nothing* is like that these days. The retirement age has gone up to sixty-six, I think, but people are working way beyond that – partly because they want to, partly because they need to. At the same time, a whole generation is having to change careers in middle age or later, learn new skills, adapt to new challenges.

We need kids today to be ready for that, and for a career path that might take them down all sorts of roads in a lifetime. We also need to frame that positively – you will have a life full of variety and opportunity if you work hard and keep your eyes open. There's no need at all for this to be a gloomy message. The opposite, actually.

So we're all actors now?

Not literally, of course. But in the sense that modern life probably has more auditions than it used to. It's nothing to be afraid of, though. The way to think of it is: I might do two or three completely different things in my career. What will they be? What would you *like* them to be?

What did you like so much about Chris Nolan?

I knew he was talented, of course, but, as I got to know him, I quickly had a hunch that he was going to be one of the great directors of the century. I always say he's the David Lean of his generation, a creator of inspired epic movies. But we also shared a love of John Huston. He was obsessed by *The Man Who Would Be King* and *The Treasure of the Sierra Madre*, and he has quite a lot in common with John.

There's this quiet confidence he radiates – it has much more authority than someone who shouts and rages. He'll ask you to do another take very calmly and without frustration. That level of poise is very rare in any business and it reflects a lot of years spent thinking deeply about what he does. It's how he's achieved such respect in the movie business and the wider world.

For all his success, he isn't flashy at all. Just this presence on set with his long coat and his flask of tea. He drinks gallons of the stuff!

And – like Huston – he devotes a lot of thought to casting?

Yes. It's a rare talent, actually, and it makes life on set so much easier. A lot of the work is done before the first take. He spends a long while thinking through who would be perfect for this or that role, and how all the people will connect once the camera is rolling. It's an art in itself.

Christian Bale was a natural for Bruce Wayne, this complex guy who is wrestling with his demons and becomes Batman. And then Gary Oldman as Jim Gordon, who's only a sergeant in the first movie and becomes Gotham's police commissioner in *The Dark Knight* (2008). Morgan Freeman, who's a good friend of mine, came on board as Lucius Fox, who runs the secret technology division at Wayne Enterprises. And there was Cillian Murphy, Katie Holmes, Liam Neeson. Amazing cast.

Chris has this ability to build a sort of rep company around him. His wife, Emma Thomas, is a fantastic producer, and together they create these huge worlds with the very best people. We filmed on location in Chicago, which was a new city for Shakira and me. Gotham is usually seen as the comic book version of New York, but Chris decided that the skyline and architecture in Chicago would make an interesting change, and it really did.

Back home, the sets at Shepperton – where I spoke my first ever lines in a movie, *A Hill in Korea* (1956) – and Cardington were just breathtaking. The scale of the movie was extraordinary. Here was a director really shifting up a gear.

How did you prepare for the role of Alfred Pennyworth?

The English butler is a familiar figure in fiction and movies. You can play him as a Jeeves, if you like, very refined and superior. Everyone remembers John Gielgud in *Arthur* (1981). But I thought, in this narrative setting, Alfred needed to be very tough indeed – he was Bruce Wayne's protector and his mentor, but also his ally. You had to believe that he would go along with this incredibly dangerous secret life that Bruce had decided upon.

Remember, this version of the Batman story is not cartoonish at all. It has wit and humour, of course, but the dark side and the pain are real. So Alfred's involvement in Bruce's secret work has to be credible. I gave him the backstory of an SAS sergeant, who's been injured and run the mess – that's how the Wayne family came to employ him as a butler. He cares deeply about Bruce and wants him to be happy, but there's no question that he's a trained killer too. He has the ambivalence of a father who knows that his adopted son has a mission in life that is also full of deadly risk.

Does he speak for the audience too?

Yes, this was a deliberate strategy that Chris and I worked up. Alfred is Bruce's moral compass and also the voice of the audience saying, 'Hold on, what are you doing now?' The Tim Burton *Batman* movies had been quite surreal and larger-than-life, but Chris's version required people to *believe* in what they were seeing. That's why Bruce's training with the League of Shadows has to be so hard – you understand how this rich orphan was taught to be such a lethal vigilante.

And, later in the story, Alfred is up to his eyes in it all, even if a big part of him just wants Bruce to let go of the quest for revenge for his parents' death and to have a happy life. He understands that this young man is going to have to make Gotham safe, at least in his own eyes, and defeat all the villains before he can even think of that.

So Alfred is emotionally invested in the whole story?

Yes, and you see that most poignantly in the third movie in the trilogy, *The Dark Knight Rises* (2012), when he thinks he's failed Bruce and his parents. He breaks down with the emotion of it all. He's tough but full of heart. Which made him a really interesting character to play across three big movies.

Did you enjoy working with Heath Ledger?

Yes, he was a lovely guy, very gentle and unassuming. I wondered how he was going to play the Joker, especially as Jack Nicholson's take had been so iconic. Brilliantly, Heath ramped up the character's psychotic side rather than going for one-liners. His Joker was deeply, deeply warped and damaged, though you never find out exactly why, or what he's really looking for.

As Alfred says to Bruce, 'Some men just want to watch the world burn.' And that was Heath's version of the character: the smeared make-up, the weird hair, the strange voice. It was chilling. Absolutely floored me the first time I saw him in action – I was terrified!

It was a total contrast to Heath Ledger's personality in real life, though?

Chalk and cheese. He and Christian were good friends and always having fun together. And then he was transformed into this scheming monster, driving a whole city towards mayhem.

Looking back, I think Heath's excellence made all of us raise our game. The psychological battle between the Joker and Batman is completely riveting. Are they in any way the same? What nudges one man to do good, and the other to do evil? The Joker wants to torment Bruce by convincing him that they're two of a kind.

It must have been a terrible shock when he died.

It was absolutely awful, it still makes me sad to think of it, more than fifteen years on. An accidental overdose, just tragic. Heath was only twenty-eight when he passed away. I hadn't even made *Zulu* when I was that age. You think of what he might have gone on to achieve, it's just heart-breaking. We were all terribly shocked, and it made doing the publicity for *The Dark Knight* that summer much more intense, because all the journalists wanted to talk about his death.

I was so pleased when he was awarded the posthumous Oscar, because it must have been at least some sort of comfort for his poor family. The truth is, we'd all hoped he would win an Academy Award and thought he should, even while we were still filming the movie. So it was just a very sad thing that he wasn't around to accept it in person. It's a performance for the ages, and even though his career was cut short so soon, he'll be remembered as a great actor, I believe.

And you made The Prestige *(2006) with Chris Nolan between* Batman Begins *and* The Dark Knight?

Yes, that's one of my favourites. It's about these two magicians in 1890s London – Robert Angier, played by Hugh Jackman, and Christian as Alfred Borden. I played John Cutter, who's a stage engineer working with both men. It was great to work with Hugh, who I think is a fantastic actor and can do anything. Multi-talented barely covers it! And Scarlett Johansson was in it as well, who is great fun and a superb actor. Plus David Bowie as Nikola Tesla, very reserved and formal in this role. Again, classic Chris, bringing together a first-rate cast as the basis of everything else.

The Prestige, which Chris co-wrote with his brother Jonathan – or Jonah, as he is called – is all about sleight of hand, and you do a lot of double takes the first time you watch the movie. The rivalry between the two magicians is presented to you inside this puzzle box. Lots of mind games, and Chris's fascination with science is in there, too. There's this whole idea of showmanship and technique, and which matters more. Which is a very important question for any storyteller, whether it's a conjuror, director or actor.

Does Nolan deliberately set out to do complicated movies?

Yes and no. People often ask me about what this or that movie of his is about, and I say, 'It's about two hours.' He loves to intrigue the audience and make them think. It's a positive feature of his films – this love of pushing you to work out what the story is saying. Sometimes it's deliberately ambiguous, and the viewer is left to make up their own minds. Other times there is an answer to the riddle. The breadcrumbs are there, if you care to look.

There are huge discussions online about his movies, with fans arguing about their precise meaning.

Is that so? I prefer just to enjoy his films and, if something is unresolved or open to interpretation, that's fine by me. It's good that somebody can make spectacular box office movies that also make the audience think a bit. Chris has shown that you can consistently produce great escapist entertainment that is also packed full of ideas. Look at his body of work already – he's not even fifty-five. There's nobody like him.

What was it like developing this great creative partnership with a director of his talent?

Oh, fantastic. We did eight movies together, if you include one voiceover, and he's probably the director I've enjoyed working with most. It was a great gift to be handed this bonus act in my career. And he's been kind enough to call me his 'lucky charm'. Well, I could say the same of him.

If there's a lesson in it all, it is that life often has plans for you that you'd never predict. Don't forget, I'd thought twice before that my career might be drawing to a close – after *Educating Rita* and then again in the early Nineties. On both occasions, I was wrong, and so it proved again when Chris came along.

It cuts both ways, though. You have to still be hungry for the experience and the work when the opportunities arise. I could have turned down Jack when he offered me a part in *Blood and Wine*. And I could have politely declined Chris's offer, too. But it didn't really occur to me to do so! In both cases, I knew immediately that I wanted to carry on.

You have to be very honest with yourself. I'm happily retired from acting now, but I gave it a great deal of thought and made sure that I was absolutely fine with the decision – which I was, and am.

Being Chris Nolan's 'lucky charm' means working on all sorts of projects, doesn't it?

It certainly does. *Inception* (2010) is a really good example – a film people are still arguing about, or so I'm told!

Definitely. Especially about the ending, when the audience isn't sure if we're watching a dream or reality.

The key concept isn't that difficult to get your head round. Basically, Leonardo DiCaprio plays a sort of thief of the mind, Dom Cobb, who infiltrates people's consciousness to steal secrets. I play his father-in-law and teacher, Professor Stephen Miles, whose daughter, Mal, has died – and Leo's character is still in deep mourning for her. Miles is a scholar at the school of architecture in Paris, and he's in touch with Dom's kids. The challenge is whether Dom can *implant* ideas as well as steal them. If he can, there's a chance he'll be reunited with his children.

You can enjoy *Inception* as an action-packed heist movie with a great cast: Cillian again, Tom Hardy, Ken Watanabe, Joseph Gordon-Levitt, Marion Cotillard as Mal, the list goes on. And you can also try and get your head around the deeper levels on which it operates and all the questions about time and reality. It's a gripping thriller as well as a movie about complicated ideas. I really like the way Chris is able to smuggle all these deep questions into a film that is also a great Saturday night outing.

Your character has to do a lot of heavy lifting in explaining the ideas.

Yes, and Chris worked really hard to edit those scenes so they are just the right length. He knows that he has to keep the pace up, even as we're introducing the audience to mind-bending possibilities. He deliberately left it all ambiguous, which I liked very much. It's true to life, which is full of ambiguities! As serious as the movie is, there's a playfulness there, too. He wants to keep the audience on its toes.

You were also the great explainer in Interstellar *(2014).*

I was – though this time, my character, a NASA scientist called Professor John Brand, is more explicitly flawed. The Earth is dying and Brand sends Cooper, who's played by Matthew McConaughey, off with a crew through a wormhole to find inhabitable planets. Meanwhile, he's trying to figure out how to transport what survives of humanity to somewhere new. And Cooper's daughter, Murph, played by Jessica Chastain, has grown up to be a brilliant physicist who is helping Brand with his work, while her astronaut dad is off somewhere in space.

Did you have scientists helping you on set?

There was this great professor called Kip Thorne around – I heard that he wrote a whole book on the science of the movie! There was a lot of work done on what should appear on Brand's blackboards. It had to be authentic. Kip was also a resource for anyone who wanted to know more about the physics. I know Matthew spent some time with him – he was fresh from winning an Oscar for *Dallas Buyers Club* (2013) and having a great comeback of his own.

The 'McConaissance'.

Is that what it was called? I didn't know that. He was excellent, anyway. But – going back to the science – I think all the quantum physics and relativity and stuff about black holes was beyond most of us. I remember Stephen Hawking coming along to the European premiere, though, which was definitely exciting. This was serious science fiction, not pure fantasy.

It's great to chase the scientific aspect of the movie if it interests you, but I personally see *Interstellar* as a movie about being a parent. Brand's daughter Amelia is played by the wonderful Anne Hathaway, and she's one of the astronauts with Cooper. So you have my character having sent his child off into space and Cooper leaving his own behind on Earth. And that separation is agony for all of them. They're involved in this profound attempt to save humanity, but they're also traumatised by what they're doing to the people they love most. That's something that everyone can relate to.

Again, this seemed to me what Chris is always doing. He relishes big concepts and horizons, but he always emphasises the human dimension. That's great for actors and for the audience, too. He works on this breathtaking canvas but in a way people can relate to. Brand has a secret that is destroying him that he has to confess to Murph – it was a powerful scene to shoot with Jessica.

They have late screenings of Interstellar *at the Prince Charles Cinema in Leicester Square. It's becoming this generation's 2001, I think.*

That's great to know, because some critics gave it a bit of a hard time when it came out. I always felt it would be a movie that people would end up seeing again and again as the years passed and appreciate more and more.

And then, after the science fiction, came Nolan's war epic, Dunkirk *(2017).*

My father had been at Dunkirk, so it felt personal. I still have the card he sent me for my sixth birthday from there, and a rosary that the Pope gave him in gratitude in 1944.

This time, I was the voice of a squadron leader talking to the

RAF pilot played by Tom Hardy. It was, I think, a nod to my role as Squadron Leader Canfield in a movie called *Battle of Britain* (1969). And Chris said, very kindly, that he wanted me to be in all of his films. We left it for people to spot – and they did!

You also had a scene in Nolan's time-travel thriller, Tenet *(2020).*

Yes, I play Sir Michael Crosby, who's a top-level British spook. He meets John David Washington's character, the hero of the movie, in a posh club for lunch. There's a good line: 'Save the world, then we'll balance the books.' I enjoyed that.

I think *Tenet* is a superb action movie – it came out in the middle of the pandemic, between lockdowns, when people were still staying away from cinemas. It did okay, but not as well as it deserved to. That was a very difficult time, obviously, for the whole movie industry. I've heard people speak warmly of it when they look back – it was great to have a big tent-pole movie like that to go to, after everyone had been stuck inside.

That was a moment when it looked like the big movie chains might go under. It was a close call, wasn't it?

Very close. Movies are a great production line that starts in the head of whoever dreams up the story, and goes via the actors and director, all the technical people, the editing and post-production, the distribution, the publicity. If any link in that chain breaks, it can't function.

The question was: would people go back to the movies after lockdown? Or was cinema as we know it finished? As it turned out, they *have* gone back – or a lot of them have. But there's still more to be done to win them all back. I hope it works out, because there is still nothing to beat the experience of going to the movies.

I can remember the days when it was quite normal to see a sign outside a cinema saying: 'House full'. That's what we have to carry on aiming for.

Do you think culture and the arts get a fair shake from government?

Not always. It's certainly true that the return from a very small investment can be huge for a country like Britain. Our film industry is one of the best in the world, and the more appealing it can be made for moviemakers to come here, in terms of tax incentives, the better.

But, in the end, the public are the people who decide, at least as far as movies are concerned. If they don't go to the cinema, the business won't work, and film making will be something very different and *much* smaller.

After eight movies with Christopher Nolan, what made you pass on Oppenheimer *(2023)?*

I didn't pass on *Oppenheimer* as such. Chris doesn't really discuss his movies in advance, that's not how he works. The thing is, I was thinking about calling it a day as an actor and focusing on writing. So I told him my thoughts, said, 'Enough is enough,' and wished him all the very best with everything. He was typically understanding and supportive of my plans. We'd had a glorious run together.

I loved what he did with *Oppenheimer*, of course. He had always been fascinated by the creation of the atomic bomb in the Manhattan Project and he worked out a way of telling the story that was characteristically ingenious, full of time leaps back and forth. Epic, of course, but also this great exploration of one man's conscience.

He had spotted this great battle between Oppenheimer, played by Cillian, and his tormentor, Lewis Strauss, who is played by Robert Downey Jr. in the movie. It's a dazzling film and it was a big cinematic event, released on the same day as *Barbie* (2023), and making almost a billion dollars worldwide.

And – what do you know? – he went on to sweep the board at the Oscars, after being passed over many times. It was wonderful, I was so pleased for him and Cillian and Emma and all the others. Chris arranged a viewing of the film for me and my family in London. It's a masterpiece, and I'm sure he'll make many more. He's so bloody talented, I love him.

I remember there was a dinner for the movie and they wanted a group photo. I said I was quite comfortable sitting at the table, and that they had more than enough stars for the photo. And – typical Chris – he brought everyone over to the table so I could be in it! That's the kind of person he is.

He was very complimentary about you in his speech when he accepted his British Film Institute fellowship in February 2024.

He was indeed. I was very touched. It was typically generous of him.

These were his words: 'I had to go off on my own. So, okay, I haven't got Michael Caine, I'd better get Matt Damon, Robert Downey Jr., Kenneth Branagh, Emily Blunt, Florence Pugh, Josh Hartnett, Cillian Murphy, Tom Conti, and hope that all those greats would add up to one Michael Caine.'

Amazingly kind words. Shakira and I went along to the dinner, which was attended by Rishi Sunak, who was then prime minister, and he made a nice speech. And then Chris was, as you say, very generous about me in his own remarks. Cillian was the one who actually presented him with the award. It was a very special occasion.

Your collaboration with him is now a celebrated example of partnership between an actor and a director – it's been compared to, say, Martin Scorsese and Robert De Niro, Jimmy Stewart and Alfred Hitchcock, John Wayne and John Ford, or, of course, Humphrey Bogart and John Huston. What did you take away from the whole experience?

Well, that's great company to be in, for a start – I'm very flattered if people say that. As far as lessons go, I've already mentioned the importance of being ready for opportunity, whether you're seventy or seventeen. I had no idea that a single phone call with Chris would have such a big impact on that phase of my career, but it really did. You can't plan for that sort of thing. You can only be prepared.

That's also part of the point. Looking back on it, it might seem like it was all pre-ordained, and a grand strategy, but moviemaking isn't like that. You make one movie at a time. Many sequels are optioned and not made. Projects get mothballed or postponed. You can never take anything for granted.

I think that's what life is like, actually. You put one foot in front of the other, do your best, and hope what you do will be a success. We were having fun and interacting really well, and we just kept going for eight movies, with me doing parts of all kinds and Chris at the helm. There is a coming together of chance and talent and chemistry, and you go with it. It doesn't happen very often in life – in work, in relationships, in friendship – but when it does, you should treasure it.

How do you know when that kind of opportunity has arrived?

It's a combination of trust, talent and excitement. You find that you are at ease, and can be yourself, around another person. There's a professional compatibility. You get along. But – at the same time – they inspire you to be as good as you possibly can.

Actors are often perceived to be total individualists. But actually, we are only as good as those around us, those we work with. And you hope that your presence helps them as well. Most things that look entirely personal actually involve a lot of people. Writing is the same, up to a point. You do most of the work before you are at the laptop, in all the discussions and conversations you have, the things you learn about, the stories that inspire you. Then there's the editing. All creativity or building is a collaboration.

The trick in life, then, is to find collaborators of all kinds, and, if it works, stick with them. It's been an important part of my good fortune as an actor, to work so often with the right people, whether it was Cy Endfield ready to take a chance on me in *Zulu*, or Lewis Gilbert with *Alfie*, or Chris in so many movies. Or, for that matter, Ollie Parker and William Ivory presenting me with the perfect last film in *The Great Escaper*.

It's the secret sauce or the X factor that can make all the difference in your life. Trust me: you'll know it when you see it!

Kermit and me. In spite of Scrooge's scowl, I loved making
The Muppet Christmas Carol.

9

Don't Forget the Fun

Do you agree with your friend Noël Coward that 'work is much more fun than fun'?

Well, far be it from me to disagree with the Master! I know what he meant by that, though. Personally, the most fun I have is with my family and friends, when I'm with Shakira, Natasha and the grandchildren. There's nothing that gives me more pleasure than time spent with them.

But I think Noël was on to something, which is that work *should* be fun. Not frivolous or easy, but enjoyable and fulfilling. It really helps if you and the people you work with retain a healthy sense of humour. Pomposity is very boring and also, in the end, an obstacle to creativity. The best actors and directors can laugh at themselves and at everything else. People who are genuinely serious about their work also tend to see the funny side of life. It's indispensable. It keeps you sane and productive.

How does that manifest itself?

For me, it's often been a case of trying new things. I'll give you an example. I did a film with the great Mexican director Alfonso Cuarón called *Children of Men* (2006), based on a P.D. James novel. It's a very bleak thriller, set in a future when the human race is slowly dying out. Clive Owen plays this civil servant who ends up helping refugees, and you've got Julianne Moore in it and Chiwetel Ejiofor in the cast, too. Really excellent group of actors.

I play this friend of Clive's character, who's called Jasper Palmer. He's another mentor figure but, in this case, very much a hippie, beatnik sort of guy, with long hair and a joint in his hand. I only ever tried marijuana once, and it was not a success. But Jasper is a total pothead. He's turned his back on the repressive government and has a place in the woods where he grows weed.

I based him partly on my friend John Lennon – Jasper's very wise and warm and funny, even though the times in which he lives are terrible. The movie stands up well, I think, and it's deadly serious. But I had an absolute ball! My role was to remind the audience of what was being lost and sacrificed in this imagined world – laughter and friendship and love. I really enjoyed playing that part, it was just something different and unexpected.

Farming today – my grandchildren, Allegra, Miles and Taylor.

In another life I could have been very happy as a full-time gardener.

Batman Begins premiere with Niki, Shakira and Natasha.

Bonds of friendship: Sean and Micheline Connery, Roger and Luisa Moore, Shakira and me.

Future Top Gun: Shakira and me with Tom Cruise and Rebecca De Mornay, 1983.

Celestial twins. Quincy Jones and I celebrate our sixtieth birthdays.

'He's my son!' Vin Diesel and I forged an instant connection that has lasted to this day.

With two great directors, Bryan Forbes and Lewis Gilbert.

John Huston had planned to cast Clark Gable and Humphrey Bogart in *The Man Who Would Be King*. In the end, he picked Sean and me. It worked out pretty well.

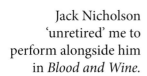

Jack Nicholson 'unretired' me to perform alongside him in *Blood and Wine*.

High on life. I based my performance as Jasper Palmer in *Children of Men* upon my friend John Lennon.

Arthurian legend: as the boss of an aristocratic spy organisation in *Kingsman*.

'Do you need some help, Master Bruce?' Alfred lends a hand in *Batman Begins*.

Genuinely startled by Heath Ledger's stunning performance as
the Joker in *The Dark Knight*.

Watch the birdie: up to all sorts of tricks in *The Prestige*.

Chris Nolan brings the gang to my table for a group photo.

I look grumpy here, but Aubrey Plaza was a terrific co-star in *Best Sellers*.

Going in Style with Morgan Freeman and Alan Arkin, the happiest movie experience I ever had.

So it's important to be serious – but not reverential?

Yes, I think so. Everybody knows how important *Zulu* was to me, and how grateful I am for the opportunities it gave to me. Well, it turned out they were planning to do a skit on the movie in *Monty Python's The Meaning of Life* (1983) – Terry Jones was directing it, and I was friendly with John Cleese. So they asked if I'd make a brief appearance in the Zulu war scene. Of course, I said yes!

Blink and you miss it, it's just a bit of fun. But it was nice to take part in the satire, to be a good sport. The Pythons were such a part of my generation's life, and this was a really good way of joining in. Turned out to be their last movie together, though I think they did some stage shows more recently. I haven't seen it in ages, but people mention it quite often.

Is that comedy part of the spirit of the Sixties that survives?

I hope so. I think the Pythons just got in under the wire – their TV show began in 1969, as I remember. But they definitely captured the wit and fun of the Sixties and took it to next level. You have to remember how much mickey-taking the Beatles did – they were a comedy troupe as well as the greatest band in the world. Always joking about themselves and life in general – especially John. He used to introduce himself as 'John Lemon'!

I think it's essential, actually. People who stay buttoned-up about what they do, and can't see the funny side of life, really do tend to be miserable. I always think of Sandra Bullock in this context – the night before she won the Best Actress Oscar, she turned up to accept her Golden Raspberry Award for some terrible movie she'd been in. That's completely the right attitude.

Absolutely nobody has a perfect score card. Everybody makes mistakes – in fact, something's gone wrong if you don't. It shows you're being too cautious, too wary of risk. What makes the difference is how you deal with failure, how you get its measure, and move on. If you can make a joke about it and show you don't take yourself too seriously, you're a winner in my book.

Do you think people worry too much about the perfect score card?

I do, especially as there's no such thing! It's good for kids to work hard for qualifications and so on, but I think that sometimes the pressure on them to get perfect grades is excessive.

Young people shouldn't be taught that, if they stumble, they've got no chance – because it's just not true at all. The more important thing is to teach them what to do *when* they stumble, how to get back up and get on with life. Constantly worrying about your ranking on social media or whatever isn't going to help, either.

Everybody needs to step back sometimes, take a deep breath and have a bit of a laugh. I love that line: 'Nothing matters very much and most things don't matter at all.' It doesn't mean that you don't strive for success or stop being ambitious. It just means that you keep a sense of perspective and a sense of humour, and make sure you have people in your life who'll encourage you to do so.

Working with the Muppets is pretty good for the soul, I'd imagine.

I loved doing *The Muppet Christmas Carol* (1992). I had no idea at the time that it would become a classic Christmas movie. They just asked me, and I was very happy to do it, to play Scrooge alongside Kermit and Miss Piggy and the rest of them.

It was like working with real actors – they really knew how to keep the pace up. But now, more than thirty years later, that movie still gets shown every year, like *It's a Wonderful Life*. It meant that all my grandchildren knew exactly what I did. And children everywhere recognise me as Scrooge!

How did you prepare for such an unusual experience as an actor?

Well, I already knew Frank Oz, who plays Fozzie Bear and Miss Piggy, from *Dirty Rotten Scoundrels*. But I realised that my role in the movie, amid all the Muppet mayhem, was to play it dead straight. I went off and looked into financial villainy a bit, so I'd get Scrooge just right. That's how that kind of comedy works, and I really enjoyed being part of it. There's a reason that the Muppets have lasted so long and why everyone still knows the characters. The people who came up with it were just geniuses, and so imaginative.

You also joined in the fun on the third Austin Powers movie.

Yes, *Goldmember* (2002). The whole series was a send-up of the Sixties, and the fashion, and all the psychedelic stuff. Just lampooning the whole decade in the best possible way. So Mike Myers asked me to play Nigel Powers, Austin's dad, and it was just too good an opportunity to pass up.

I loved doing that movie, poking fun at the Sixties but also celebrating it all again. It was great fun. I remember doing the scene where I had to tell Dr Evil's henchmen exactly how to fight me: 'Judo chop! Judo chop!'

Beyoncé was one of your co-stars, too.

She was – she played Foxxy Cleopatra. Only nineteen at the time, I think, and a very nice person. You could already tell how focused she was and how big a star she was going to be. I remember the first day on set, I asked her what her ambition was, and she said, 'I want to win an Academy Award for a movie.' Not a trace of arrogance, just clarity.

She was nominated a couple of years ago.

I'm sure she'll win an Oscar eventually. She's already won a bunch of Grammys!

More than thirty.

Exactly. Phenomenal achievement. But on set she was totally engaged in the comedy, as we all were – Michael York and Robert Wagner, and the late Verne Troyer, who played Mini-Me so brilliantly. Mike Myers is a sort of crazy genius, and a lovely guy, who kept us all laughing and enjoying ourselves. I remember him playing loud rock'n'roll between takes, which was a new one on me! He knew a lot about my movies and couldn't have been more charming to me. I had a really good time.

More recently, you also played a spy in Kingsman: The Secret Service *(2014).*

Yes, that was directed by Matthew Vaughn, who's very talented. Again, the cast was fantastic – Colin Firth, Mark Strong, Samuel L. Jackson and Taron Egerton, who was still in his twenties but already going places. It's an action-comedy thriller, not as absurd as *Goldmember*, but still great fun. I played Arthur, who's the head of this secret spy organisation founded by aristocrats. It was a funny twist – about as far from Harry Palmer as it's possible to get!

I guess Taron's character, Eggsy, who's very working-class in the movie, has more in common with Harry. I liked the fact that they gave him glasses once he became a spy. It felt like a nod to *The Ipcress File*.

You love football and you're a Chelsea supporter. Have you always followed the game?

Well, I took a long break from actually going to matches. When I was six, my dad took me to see Millwall play, and someone threw an empty beer bottle and it hit me on the head. After that, I didn't go to a football match again for quite a few years.

I was in the King's Road one Saturday lunchtime and Richard Attenborough was there – we'd just done *A Bridge Too Far* together. He said, 'Are you going to see Chelsea, Michael?'

I said, 'No, the reason I don't go to football is this' – and I told him the story about being walloped on my head on the terraces.

So Richard said, 'Look, come to the match today, come with me.'

I said, 'You're really going to see Chelsea now?'

And he said, 'Michael, I'm on the board of the directors!'

So off we went to Stamford Bridge. I think he ended up as the club's life president – they did a lovely tribute to him when he died about ten years ago.

After that, I used to go whenever I could. I took Shakira once – I think she enjoyed it! But these days I'm mostly happy watching the game on a huge flat screen. The bigger the better.

The quality of the picture is amazing now, it's been great for sports fans.

Did you play?

I played a lot of football at school – right back, that was my position – and it really helped because I'd had rickets. Running around was very good for me. It's good for everyone – I used to do bits and bobs for the National Playing Fields Association, because I think every child should have space to be healthy and let off steam. When I was a bit more mobile, I used to love nothing more than a kickabout in the garden with my grand-kids. Taylor, my elder grandson, is an excellent player and used to live in his kit – but I think he's more inclined to be a DJ now. We bought him the equipment he needs, it's quite technical!

And you were in action on the pitch for Escape to Victory.

Yes – with Pelé and Bobby Moore and the rest of them! Quite an experience. You realise just how good the best players are when you're that close to them on the pitch. They were incredible.

You were also well known for organising games of scratch cricket on set.

That's true. Gary Oldman used to tease me when we were making the Batman movies – he said I nailed my lines so I could get back to the cricket as soon as possible! I always love the arrival of spring when the season gets going. It's part of being English, I suppose.

I remember Gary Oldman saying in an interview that he was amazed by how you got it right take after take.

That means a lot coming from an actor of his stature. He's remarkable. He can do anything: Jim Gordon, Dracula, Harry Truman, Winston Churchill. Another working-class Londoner who has done a lot of movies.

Many of your friends have been big golf players. Did that not appeal to you?

It's not my cup of tea. Morgan Freeman's a great golfer, and so was Johnny Gold. I mean, some of my friends did their best to show me how to play. Sidney Poitier had the patience of a saint, but even he nearly lost it trying to teach me. Sean Connery *did* lose it! He was a really committed golf player, having learned the game for that famous scene in *Goldfinger*. And he would find a way to play wherever he was in the world.

Well, Sean just couldn't understand why I couldn't grasp the basics, no matter how hard he tried to show me. In the end, he actually grabbed one of my clubs and snapped it in two. You don't forget that kind of thing in a hurry! I took it as a sign that my destiny did not lie on the links. Which was fine – I had plenty of other things to do.

What sort of things?

I've always loved cooking – that was one of the reasons I was drawn to the restaurant business. I think my generation that lived through the war has a very particular relationship with food. We were very lucky in my family, because we escaped rationing when we were evacuated to the countryside and ate very good local produce. But rationing didn't end completely until 1954 and even then it was Lyons Corner Houses, fish and chips, pretty standard stuff.

When new restaurants opened up in the Sixties – less stuffy, and also better – people like me got our first taste of fine dining and really embraced it. Suddenly, London was full of coffee bars, and French, Italian, Indian and Chinese restaurants. It all happened so quickly.

How did you learn to cook?

From necessity to start with – which then turned into genuine enthusiasm. Remember, I was a bachelor for many years, so I pretty much had to look after myself. When I was living with Terry Stamp, I think the first thing I mastered was egg custard! And I took it from there.

My first stay in Paris when I was a young man was also a revelation – I discovered that you could eat very well indeed, quite cheaply. I particularly remember La Coupole on the Boulevard du Montparnasse – a fantastic place, that was really the model for Langan's.

All of that played into the way I portrayed Harry Palmer, especially in *The Ipcress File*. It helped that Len Deighton himself was a great cook – and if you look at the interior of Harry's kitchen in the movie, you can see some of the cookery comic strips Len used to do for the *Observer* on the walls.

Cooking is a great thing to learn how to do – like everything, it's all in the preparation, getting the right ingredients, knowing what utensils you need, how long to cook things, how high a temperature. Mastering the basics, so you can go on and be ambitious and move up to more advanced recipes.

I remember Danny Kaye being a great cook in LA, and making fantastic Chinese meals in his kitchen, with the help of a chef. I used to go along quite often to those evenings. You'd bump into Cary Grant or Prince Philip!

Cooking is very relaxing, too. I'm not one for psychotherapy – I prefer practical distractions. Being busy in the kitchen or at the barbecue is a good way of spending time on your own and not brooding – doing something useful and absorbing. I practised my lines when I was cooking, too, to see if I really knew them.

Gardening is also a great passion of yours. Where did that come from?

Well, we had a little garden when I was growing up, but there wasn't a lot of greenery in my life until we were evacuated. I think living in the countryside had a lasting impact upon me. I never wanted to farm, but I did love the idea of having a big garden and growing things.

Were you ever drawn by the idea of self-sufficiency?

Yes, it was an idea that was gaining ground in the Seventies. Being an actor, especially from a working-class background, you always worry in the back of your mind that, for whatever reason, you'll have to feed your family yourself one day. Once we bought Mill House, I spent a lot of my spare time turning those five acres into a proper garden, getting rid of the stinging nettles.

I planted loads of vegetables so we could eat our own produce at home. And a lot of trees, too. I'd buy them when they were already thirty-five feet high, so we could enjoy them straight away! And I did love building a bridge.

We were on the riverfront back then, and all these tourist boats would float past. You'd hear this voice from a loudspeaker: 'And on the left, the gentleman mowing the lawn with the glasses on is Mr Michael Caine!' In the end, I planted enough fir trees so I had a spot of privacy. But it made me chuckle.

It's very peaceful, gardening. You feel you're stepping back in time a bit, getting back to basics, with the English seasons – which I missed in Hollywood – and different kinds of soil, and learning about which plant needs what kind of tending. It's very rewarding, especially creating a garden from scratch. Good exercise, too, especially digging. In another life, I could have been very happy as a full-time gardener. It's endlessly fascinating. I built up my own library of gardening books, I had whole shelves of them. I knew the Latin names of plants, the whole nine yards.

Each garden you create must be like a great movie you have been part of.

It is – probably even more personal, because it's just you making this special place to share with your family and friends. And, if you're superstitious, which actors generally are, you can spot all sorts of things in a garden.

When we were thinking of buying our place in Surrey, I looked around the grounds and thought how much I'd enjoy working on it. Suddenly, I looked up and there was a flock of amazing parrots in the sky! I asked the foreman and he told me that they were Brazilian parrots that had escaped from Shepperton during the filming of *The African Queen* (1951) – John Huston and Humphrey Bogart again! I'm not a mystical person, but if that wasn't a sign, then I don't know what is.

Do you have a favourite garden?

Well, I love the Royal Horticultural Society's garden at Wisley in Surrey. And Shakira and I have always enjoyed the Chelsea Flower Show. It's something you can share with your friends, too – I used to love talking about gardening to my great friend, Bryan Forbes, who directed me in *The Wrong Box* (1966) and *Deadfall* (1968).

Bryan really had green fingers and we used to swap tips. I remember him teasing me about how many different kinds of potato I was growing! I miss him, but we still see his wife Nanette Newman. And their daughter Sarah is married to Johnnie Standing, who was so good in *The Great Escaper*.

What about cars?

The truth is, I'd never bothered to take my test. But I pretty much knew how to drive from all the close-up shots in *The Italian Job* when I was driving the car. Anyway, when we moved to Hollywood in 1979, I decided I should take the test properly. There was a woman in charge of the whole process and she said, 'Now, you will not have any conversation with the examiner, blah, blah, blah' – all the rules and regulations.

And I said, 'Thank you, ma'am.'

So I got in the car and the examiner looked at me and said, 'I loved you in *The Man Who Would Be King*!' And I passed.

177

Did you buy a lot of cars?

It was never one of my main enthusiasms, no. I did have a gorgeous Rolls-Royce Silver Shadow two-door drophead coupe. It was the first car I bought and the insurance was so expensive it would have been cheaper to pay for a chauffeur. It appeared in the documentary *Candid Caine* (1969), but I didn't actually drive it.

I do remember that the first showroom I visited in Berkeley Square was very snobbish. I wound them up by reading out my shopping list: 'Milk, bread, newspaper, cigarettes, Rolls-Royce.' That didn't go down at all well, and I was slung out on my ear. But I did go back another day in pretend-Jack Carter mode to give them a piece of my mind!

Anyway, I sold that Roller to a restaurant owner called Jack Leach in 1970. It still pops up at auction – I think somebody bought it for about £120,000 last year! More than half a century after I owned it, and it is still somehow associated with me. Funny, really.

I've never been a petrolhead. Look at all the cars that were destroyed in *The Italian Job*! That was great fun. I *did* have a voice part in *Cars 2* (2011) as Finn McMissile, a cool Aston Martin who's a British spy.

What's it like doing voiceover work for animated movies?

Oh, lots of fun. That movie, which was made by Pixar, was the first 3D film I'd ever done, and technically amazing. Plus, it introduced my voice to another generation of kids, which was lovely. You go in and do your bit in the script in a couple of days, and that's it, it's very straightforward. I liked doing it.

Your reputation as a good sport was enhanced by the Madness song, 'Michael Caine', to which you contributed a few spoken lines. It came out in 1984, but people still play it.

Do they? I wasn't going to do it and then Natasha persuaded me to – she must have been about eleven at the time, and she loved Madness. I just had to say 'I am Michael Caine' in my Harry Palmer voice a few times, it wasn't a lot of work. You can hear me at the end saying, 'I think we got it there, don't you?' or something like that. That's the unpredictable thing about pop music, the stuff that lasts and the stuff that doesn't. When I was doing it, it never occurred to me that it would have such a long life. But I'm glad it has. It's a good track.

You've always loved music, haven't you?

Absolutely, it was such a part of my early career and all the excitement of the times. And then there was the disco era, which I really enjoyed – they called me 'Disco Michael'! It was a sort of ritual. We'd all go out dancing and then head off for Italian food afterwards. The English restaurants had all closed by that time of night, and they weren't as good anyway.

How did you get into mixtapes?

I always loved making them – this was in the era of cassette tapes to start with. Then I moved on to discs. I must have made thousands of them over the years. It's a fun thing to do, especially if you're travelling a lot. And it's a nice thing to share with people. I enjoy being a secret DJ for my friends!

I think it was around 2006 that I was having dinner with Elton John in Nice and I recognised some of the music he was playing – Sarah McLachlan and Eva Cassidy. I told Elton about my compilations, and, to my delight, he was really enthusiastic. He put in a call to the boss of Universal, Lucian Grainge, which led to me releasing a CD called *Cained*.

What sort of tracks did you pick?

Well, this is a while ago now. But there was a great mix of Nina Simone's 'Sinnerman' and Chicane's 'No Ordinary Morning' was on it, too. A track by Doctor Rockit, as well. It was all about the beat and the mood.

What did you like about chill-out music?

The clue is in the name! Chill music was really started by Claude Challe in the Buddha Bar in Paris. Very romantic, very atmospheric. I've always believed in the importance of ambience – it's a word I used a lot on the set of the Harry Palmer movies.

I love listening to music at home, relaxing, and enjoying all the artistry and curation that goes into it. Chill music is a terrific genre, very hard to do well. Some people confuse it with background music or 'muzak', but it's much more sophisticated than that. It has to create a particular mood, like all good music. I had hundreds of CDs and then got into downloading tracks when all that got going.

Again, very much a cultural moment: this was when everyone was swapping playlists for their iPods, which still seemed very new.

That's right, and my friends would download my latest lists from my computer. For me, it was about the music rather than the technology. I have heard the chill-out style called 'Balearic' and other things, but I just listened out for tracks that would fit together and make a great compilation. Plus, it was amusing to be putting out a chill-out CD as an actor in his seventies! It's fun to keep people guessing and to show a bit of versatility.

Given that you love and collect music, was it difficult to choose eight records for Desert Island Discs *in 2009?*

Oh, yes, very. I narrowed it down and narrowed it down. It's an honour to go on that show and people do listen back to past episodes, so I wanted to get it right.

It was broadcast at Christmas, so it was natural to have John Lennon's 'Happy Xmas (War is Over)', and Elgar's 'Nimrod' and Sinatra's 'My Way' were easy to pick, too. But I snuck Chicane in there and Elbow, whom I'd seen on television when they were playing Glastonbury. Wonderful music.

And you chose Ayn Rand's The Fountainhead *(1943) as your book. Why was that?*

Well, it's one of the great modern novels. People read too much into the politics of it, which interested me less than the architecture. The main character, Howard Roark, is an architect and I think if I hadn't been an actor I'd have loved to have been involved in architecture. It's a fascinating thing to do.

Also, my elder daughter is named after the heroine in the book, Dominique Francon.

Curiosity is a big part of your character, isn't it?

It is, for all sorts of reasons. If you were becoming an adult in the post-war years, you had a natural appetite for new things and new experiences. That's really what the Sixties was – an explosion of curiosity!

And that was doubly so for people from a working-class background. Suddenly, it was possible to experience everything, to travel, to try new things. The worst thing about class is the way it can confine people's expectations and dreams.

What William Blake called 'mind forg'd manacles'.

That's it exactly. Well, we were breaking free of all that, and about time, too. So all these enjoyable things we're discussing – I was determined to try them all. And if I do something, I like being a bit obsessive about it, treating it as a skill to master or a new kind of knowledge to pick up. That makes it even more enjoyable.

Another element to it is that actors lead a stop-go life as far as their work is concerned. You have the intense time on a shoot and then you're suddenly waiting for the next movie, which may be booked in your diary but not for a while. So how you fill the intervening time is important. There's a big difference between fun and idleness. I like to keep busy.

Do all these other interests help you ground yourself?

Oh, yes. I've always insisted on defining myself and being myself. The things I do outside acting, and that I enjoy, are a big part of that. When you've got a trowel in your hand and you're checking on your potato crop, you forget about Hollywood! Or trying to get a roast just right. It reminds you that you're just a normal person who has had a very fortunate life, enjoyed success, but hasn't been changed fundamentally by it. I don't think I have been.

How do you feel when people describe you as an icon or a screen legend?

I take it kindly, of course. Who wouldn't? But I don't take it, or myself, so seriously. I think it's a terrible thing that can befall famous people, and you have to remember that I was there from the start, when the Beatles were becoming the most famous people on the planet. They handled it by never forgetting their Liverpudlian roots.

Me too, as a working-class Londoner – when I became well known, I was delighted to enjoy the rewards for which I'd worked. But I knew perfectly well that I was still the same person, and, crucially, that fame is fickle. It ebbs and flows like the tide.

Everyone has their equivalent in life – the thing for which they are best known, on whatever scale. It's good to earn your reputation in absolutely any field, for your hard graft to be recognised by your peers, or your customers, or whoever your audience is. You can be a brilliant businessman, or a fantastic carer, or an inspiring teacher, or make the best cup of tea in your neighbourhood. And, if so, terrific.

But you have to be level-headed and remember that everything has its season, and what really makes a difference in a life is the fulfilment you yourself derived from your work and the love you gave to your family and friends. That's what will last – not fame, which is fleeting, by definition.

Hence the importance of fun.

Life *is* fun, and I think some people forget that. It stays fun, if you deal with the hard stuff in the right way. I mean, as you know, when I got home from Korea I collapsed with malaria! So it wasn't all easy. But I stayed the same. I was still a young cockney boy who wanted to make the most of his life and wanted to be an actor. I got on with it.

That remains my philosophy seventy years later. I try to enjoy every day as much as possible. I count my blessings, especially the great good fortune of family and friends. I am never complacent, but I am a very happy man.

Keeping Big Tech in perspective. Harry Palmer plays it cool
in *Billion Dollar Brain*.

10

The Michael Caine Emoji:
How to Handle Modern Life

You were born in the Depression and we are talking as the first quarter of the twenty-first century heads to a close. You're on your twenty-first prime minister and your fifth monarch. How much has changed in that time?

Everything and nothing! Or to put it another way, human nature is a constant and, as everything changes around us, it's important to remember that the basics remain the same: work, fun, love, family, friends. The question is how you adapt to each new phase in your life, and how you protect your key values, while remaining open to new things.

That philosophy of life seems to lie behind your approach to technology.

It does. I really enjoy new gadgets almost as much as Peter Sellers used to. He was the first person I knew with an answering machine and – typically of Peter – his message was him doing an impression of me! He started all that off.

I have an Apple Watch, which tells me all sorts of things, and I use my iPad for just about everything – from work on my writing to checking the Test match scores. But it's just a fantastic tool. It's not my window onto the world, as I think phones have become for too many people. I leave it at home when we go out without a second thought. Whereas I see some people who have lost their phones, or forgotten to bring them, and it's like watching addicts looking for a fix. It's totally out of balance.

Are you surprised by how much the digital revolution has changed life?

It depends upon how you look at it. Funnily enough, the third Harry Palmer movie, *Billion Dollar Brain*, which came out more than fifty years ago, predicted a sort of super-computer that could, in theory, start uprisings in foreign countries and disrupt everything around the world.

There's this deranged cold warrior in Texas called General Midwinter, who's an oil tycoon, and he spends all this money on this huge electronic system at his HQ. He tells Harry that the 'Brain' he has built 'makes the Pentagon look like a room at the Alamo!' And he's organised a private army to wage war on the Soviet bloc, starting in Latvia.

It's escapism, of course, but that movie almost predicted what's happening now, with all the worries about Big Tech and the power of social media, and private armies, and the rest of it.

The thing is, I think we need to take a leaf out of Harry's book and keep it all in perspective. Machines and robots are only as bad as the people programming them, and that should be our focus. They are what we make of them, that's all.

You mean that people are behaving a bit too passively, as though they had no say in the questions posed by new technology?

Yes, and that's always been true. You have to remember – the television was an astonishing device when it started to arrive in everyone's homes. And, no question, TV did change everything, not least in its impact upon movies. But movies have survived. That tells you something.

Every generation is a bit in awe of the new technology it gets presented with. Who was it that said, maybe one day, every major city in America would have a telephone – as if it was almost unthinkable? Well, it turned out to be *completely* thinkable, pretty quickly. And now almost everyone has a mobile phone, let alone a landline in their home. My point, I guess, is that the basic questions of life haven't really changed, even as things have been made much easier for us by technology.

But there's a risk that new technology can become an obsession in itself?

I think there is. Take dating apps – now those *are* a mystery to me, but it's not for my generation and, besides, I'm a very happily married man. If people want to use them for convenience to meet people, that's fine.

But what makes a relationship work hasn't changed. You might meet someone you like online, but they're no more or less likely to be right for you than if you'd met them the traditional way. And from what I hear, the identities people present online are often very different from what they're like in real life. It's a bit of a land of make believe. And that's a recipe for disappointment. It's a bad idea to present a false picture of yourself – it'll always catch up with you. Reality bites sooner or later.

Do you think digital life can make people ungrounded?

Hard to say, as my own use of these devices is totally geared to things I would have done anyway, only less quickly. But I do get a sense that some people almost climb through the screen of their phones and forget where the real world stops and this big online world starts. And, if everyone is doing it, they tend to follow their friends, so they're not left out. There's a bit of a herd mentality to it all.

So you're not, say, a fan of Instagram?

I don't even know what that is! It doesn't really interest me. If people want to swap stories, music, video clips and jokes online, that's great. But when it becomes the centre of their lives, then it's a problem. In the end, you have to live in the real world and I'm not so sure that too much digital life is good for people in that respect.

I checked up and somebody has designed a Michael Caine emoji.

Again, whatever that is! I think all the jargon and tech-talk makes some people incomprehensible. You can't beat plain English if you want to be understood by people of all ages and backgrounds.

Look, it's good for every new generation to have its own thing. My lot had the Sixties, after all. Whatever comes next is probably going to be digital in some way or other. But it should still be about *human beings* and the things they care about. You have to keep a level head and not be too dazzled by technology, especially as it is changing so fast nowadays.

You can't eat a tweet or live in a podcast. Love is still love, work is still work, friendship is still friendship. A walk in the park is always better than an hour on the sofa playing video games. None of that changes – unless people give up the key things that have made us human since history began.

I don't expect they will give them up, in fact. I think all this will settle down as we figure out how to make it work for *us*, rather than the other way round.

When you started as an actor, ITV had only just been launched and the BBC dominated television. Now there are all the streaming services, which are making their own movies too. What do you think about the Netflix age?

Well, we watch Netflix and the rest of them, like everyone else. If it's good television, I'm interested. And the convenience of being able to watch whenever you like is nice.

What you're seeing is more and more actors making their names in television rather than the movies. People mention Elisabeth Moss a lot, that's a good example.

Yes, she's been in a run of great television series: The West Wing, Mad Men, Top of the Lake, The Handmaid's Tale. *So-called 'prestige TV'. She's won Golden Globes and Emmys.*

But she hasn't crossed my radar as a movie-lover at all, because movies aren't really what she prioritises. Which is fine, good luck to her. But it's a new thing to have actors trying to be stars *just* on TV. It used to be a place where movie stars got their start – Clint Eastwood made his name on the small screen in *Rawhide*. George Clooney started out playing a doctor in a TV series. Denzel Washington did the same. But once they'd got into movies, that was that. It may be that's changing.

Is that a bad thing?

Not necessarily. Variety is good. But I wouldn't want to see too much acting talent drawn away from moviemaking – the two key ingredients in successful cinema are creative talent and audience enthusiasm. If either starts to shrink, you've got a big problem.

How does the BBC fit into all this?

I've done a lot for the BBC over the years, mostly interviews. They did a nice programme a few years ago, compiling all the archive clips. I've had my differences with the BBC over the years, but I hope it survives and does well. The fact is, though, it's going to get harder and harder to make people pay the licence fee, especially youngsters who don't even own a television. They watch everything on computers and phones. So that's a big obstacle they'll have to clear somehow.

The BBC has to get its act together so it can provide certain services that aren't available commercially. That's a serious challenge in the new media world.

Are you thinking about news in particular?

Not just news – drama production is really important, too. But, yes, having a news channel that is publicly funded is a good idea. You know that you're going to get the basic facts from the BBC, even if they do make mistakes sometimes.

Are you worried about all the misinformation around – fake news and conspiracy theories?

I worry about it when people take it seriously. Look, there have always been lies and propaganda. It's as old as history. And there have always been cranks cooking up stories about plots, or faked moon landings, or UFOs. What seems to have happened is that there is a lot more of it now, being churned out by people on the internet. You can see that it's nonsense.

What happens when people don't *think it's nonsense, though? When they believe all the falsehoods they see and read online?*

Well, that's different! I grew up at a time where people got their news from a few mainstream national newspapers and the wireless. And then a small number of TV channels. Plus a thriving local press.

You knew there'd be bias, there always is – but it wasn't that hard to find out what was going on, either, because there weren't that many sources of news. They were all pretty big and professional, and you could listen and read and get a sense of what was happening in the world.

I think it's harder for the younger generation to do that with confidence. Things that are labelled 'news' on the internet often aren't news at all and spread all sorts of lies and rumours around the place. As always, it comes back to education: we're going to have to teach kids how to sift the good stuff from the bad. It's not impossible, it's just another item to add to the 'to do' list.

Part of the problem is general cynicism, isn't? I mean, about anything being true or worthwhile anymore. Can anything be done about that?

You're right about the growth of cynicism. And you can't just tell people to stop being cynical. That doesn't get you anywhere.

The antidote to cynicism is, once again, curiosity. Did you know that Albert Einstein and I share a birthday? Einstein used to describe himself as 'passionately curious'. Well, we can't all come up with the theory of relativity, obviously! But staying curious about life is a really good habit to develop.

For me personally, it's connected to my photographic memory. I can always remember things that I've read and interesting facts that I've picked up. That's why Peter Sellers came up with the catchphrase for me: 'Not a lot of people know that.' I'm not sure I ever said those actual words! But it's true that I like mentioning things that are surprising or revealing.

Inquisitiveness is a very powerful tool. Actors are always observing and, in my case, I have loved using the time between roles to read. Staying curious helps you in all sorts of ways. You develop perspective – what does this mean, what is the history that has led to it? You stay more up to date with change, because you tend to be more intrigued than threatened by new information. And it helps you stay independent. If you're curious in life, you'll know things that will undercut the pomposity of people who assume that they're superior to you or talk nonsense, thinking wrongly that you don't know enough to challenge them.

It's really important to stay enthused and in touch with the world. Apart from anything else, it makes life more enjoyable. Cynicism is a recipe for misery. Curiosity is a recipe for excitement.

Are people today too obsessed with money?

If they make it the be all and end all of their lives, then yes. Remember the old prospector in *The Treasure of the Sierra Madre*? He says to Bogart, 'I know what gold does to men's souls.' Well, I've seen that, too.

But people who say money doesn't matter are either foolish or have been born into great wealth. Nobody who has known poverty would ever say such a thing. You have to earn enough to put food on the table for your family, as my parents did. Working-class people know that every penny counts and they are willing to work very hard to provide for the people they are responsible for.

I am never impressed by attacks on successful people who have sweated for their money, as though it is somehow a bad thing. My dad died of liver cancer in his fifties and I learned years afterwards that he could have been cured if we'd had enough money. So I pay no heed to people who say that it's somehow wrong to worry about your earnings.

In that light, how should people handle financial questions when they are pursuing their dreams?

The first thing you have to do is work out how much you need to earn to provide at least the basics for your family. There should always be a level you have in mind below which you don't want to fall. If it's just you, it's up to you where that level is. But if you're looking after others, you have to be responsible and realistic.

That means that you can't be too picky about work, even if you have much higher ambitions. I did all sorts of jobs to keep the wolf from the door when I was starting out. I worked in factories, as a dishwasher, as a night clerk at a hotel, in construction. None of that diminished my dreams of being an actor. But it had to be done.

The thing you want to do may not earn you a living immediately. In fact, it almost certainly won't. When I was understudy to Peter O'Toole, I made more per week from the pinball machine than I did from the job itself!

What changes when you start to achieve your ambitions?

Well, then there are new challenges. I remember my mum literally not being able to understand the sums of money I was earning when I started doing well in movies. She didn't know how much 'a million' was. Why should she?

The thing to remember is that it's easy to lose your head. You have to make sure you've brought your values with you when you cross the border into the world of success. By which I mean: don't forget why you wanted to do this in the first place. Did you dream of having a swimming pool in your house or a fancy car? Maybe. But I bet that wasn't the main reason.

You should never apologise for doing enough work to keep your family in the lifestyle you've provided for them. I used to do three movies a year.

At the same time, don't do anything *just* for money, it's a bad idea. I've been lucky in life, I've been well paid as an actor. But I always read the script carefully and decided whether I really wanted to do it. You don't always get it right, and everyone has bills to pay. But if life is just about money, you'll be miserable.

So how do you pick and choose work?

It helps a lot if you enjoy working, which I always have done. If you make a movie that pays well but doesn't work out – on to the next one. If you keep busy, you can afford to take parts that don't pay as well but are challenging and interesting.

People often ask me why I did so many movies. The answer is that I enjoyed making them and that I got to do all sorts of films. So I might do a big movie with a big pay cheque, and then move on to a smaller film that didn't make such an impact on my bank account. Movies like *Mona Lisa* or *Last Orders*, which I loved doing.

It's a good strategy. Hard work enables you to seek out the high-quality projects *and* to take care of your family. That's the perfect combination.

What role should generosity play in life?

It should be central. It's a pleasure to share the rewards of your work with your family, friends and colleagues. I like the idea of the random act of kindness, too.

I'll give you an example. Years ago, we were in New York and we took the whole family to Nobu, which is a restaurant we all love. And at the end when I asked for the bill, they said, 'It's all taken care of.' Turned out Robert De Niro, who was one of the restaurant's founders, was treating us. Now, we don't know each other that well and we've never acted together in a movie. But he still did that. A lovely gesture.

Do you think modern life is too much about spectacle and show?

Well, it's funny. We were talking about the Met Gala the other day, and the way in which it's plastered across the news every year. All these people in Manhattan you've never heard of dressed up in ridiculous costumes!

The old Hollywood glamour was great and exciting. There have always been staged photos for movie publicity, especially at Cannes and places like that. It used to be almost an art form in itself.

But there comes a point when people are doing more and more absurd things just to attract attention. That's a bit embarrassing, really. Dignity is a big part of real glamour and I reckon people are increasingly ready to sacrifice that, just to start a buzz on social media or whatever. It really isn't my scene at all.

The whole idea of the 'influencer' is a shift from your time in the movies, isn't it?

I don't really see what it amounts to. 'Influence' comes in all sorts of forms, but it should always be earned rather than snatched. The idea that you set out in life to be an 'influencer' is very odd to me!

I suppose it's because it costs so relatively little now to start your own YouTube channel or podcast.

Yes, and I expect a few of them are good. I wouldn't know. What's bizarre is the motive – 'Oh, I want to influence people' – rather than doing something great, or making a little movie of your own, or some acting or comedy. Or whatever is your specialty. Then, the better you get, you might become influential as a *consequence* of your excellence.

The weird bit is putting the cart before the horse and making it your ambition to have influence. Well, go into politics, get elected and do some real good!

It's the old Andy Warhol line about a future where everyone would be world-famous for fifteen minutes, isn't it?

Yes, except this isn't even genuine fame. It's attention-seeking and signalling to the world that you're important because you're important. It's meaningless. And it's always a mistake to reward mediocrity, or to settle for it yourself.

No short cuts, in other words?

As a rule of thumb, I would distinguish between strokes of luck and short cuts. Everyone needs the occasional stroke of luck, and the ability to make use of it. I've certainly had my share.

But short cuts rarely exist. Sure, you can have people who inherit a business or whatever it may be, and they may start off with a more comfortable life than most. But there's no fast track to fulfilment and a sense of purpose. You have to build your own life, whether you're a prince or a pauper.

Life isn't a code you suddenly crack and then get everything you want all at once. And anyone who tells you otherwise is leading you up the garden path.

How do you make sense of the sheer complexity of modern life?

I have one great advantage, which is that I've experienced all kinds of living. I've known poverty, been in the Army, been on benefits, been rich, been rinsed by the taxman, been a businessman, been a writer. I've seen and done a lot.

That means that I can see things from all sorts of perspectives. I haven't led a working-class lifestyle for many years, but I will always understand the working-class mentality, because you never lose it, however well you do in life. I understand people who feel insecure and worried about their jobs and their kids. That doesn't change.

I haven't lost my sense of affinity with ordinary working-class youngsters starting out now. I always hope that they are being given plenty of chances in life and opportunities.

Do you think they are?

Not as much as I'd like. There's no rolling back what happened in the Sixties, which was that, suddenly, it was *possible* for someone from a working-class background to get on in life and reach the heights of any profession or activity. The door was opened and is still open.

The problem is that not enough people get to walk through it.

Why do you think that is?

A combination of things. The class system still exists but, as we've discussed, it's less obvious than it was. It's gone underground now, more nudges and winks than out-in-the-open snobbery.

You see it in big, successful cities. They're like little planets. They're expensive to live in, and they have these tight-knit networks of opportunity that are passed around between a tiny group of people. I've heard them called 'dream hoarders', which is a very good way of putting it. It's not quite a closed shop, but it's harder for some than others to get in.

What can be done to stop the 'dream hoarding'?

You have to have an education system and hiring policies that really put rocket-boosters under kids from deprived backgrounds. Are there people in their lives, at school or in their communities, who will nudge them towards success? Who is in their lives to convince them that hard graft and focus will be rewarded eventually and that they are as entitled as anyone to their dreams and ambitions?

People ask me why I've not dropped my cockney accent and have never turned my back on my roots. Well, why on earth should I? But also, I want other kids from a similar background to think, if he made it, so can I. And they can.

But the flipside of that is that they have to step up to the plate themselves. Just being angry about your lot in life won't achieve anything. There *are* victims in life, but not as many as the modern world encourages people to think! It's a really important aspect of this whole discussion – not walking into the elephant trap of self-pity and victimhood. It's a hard place to escape from once you've convinced yourself that you have no control over your own destiny, and the system has been rigged to ensure that you will fail.

For a start, it's not true. Champions and stars don't wallow in misfortune, they get up and get on with it. Apply for a job, apply for a course, get in shape, learn a skill, ask a successful person for advice and mentoring. Keep moving and trying new things. I treated myself as a one-man studio, a one-man operation, determined to do the work I wanted to by hook or by crook.

Have the patience to wait for the breakthrough, and don't expect it to come about in a predictable way – I was just about the last of my gang of actors to become famous, but it was definitely worth the wait.

While you're waiting and if things don't go right, I have a saying: *use the difficulty.* I'll give you a left-field example of using the difficulty. A few years ago, we were in New York, and I was walking down Lexington Avenue, and I literally fell into a pothole. It was a proper tumble, I needed stitches and everything. So poor Shakira rushed to see me at the hospital and she was upset, as you'd expect. I must have looked a right state.

I think everybody was expecting me to feel very sorry for myself – and then suddenly I realised, 'Hey! This is great! Now I don't have to go to bloody Paris to do movie publicity!' Which, to be honest, felt like pretty good news at the time. It's funny, looking back. I had *used the difficulty.*

It's a good practice to really examine the scene of a setback for the thing that is going to help you: nine times out of ten, it'll be there if you look hard enough. Reframe the crisis as an opportunity and turn it to your advantage, even if only slightly. Remember, you're not on your own, but at the same time, nobody is going to make it happen for you.

You're a great believer in public libraries, aren't you?

Yes, and it worries me that hundreds of them have closed in the last couple of decades. Other than the movie house, the public library was my home from home when I was growing up. It was where I encountered books like Norman Mailer's *The Naked and the Dead* (1948) and James Jones' *From Here to Eternity* (1951), stories about regular soldiers that meant something to someone of my background. Kids in my class used to call me the Professor because I loved reading so much.

I left school at sixteen with four O levels. But my real education took place in the library. It was like a paradise, my window into all these worlds – whether set in the past, the future, other countries, or completely imaginary scenarios. I didn't think of it this way at the time, but I'm sure my enthusiasm to write books has its origins in those happy hours at the local library.

It's obvious that those facilities should be a right not a privilege for kids today. For everyone, actually. I hear about the growth of digital libraries where you can download books for free and that's certainly better than nothing. But you can't beat the physical space of a library, where you can browse the shelves and take your time choosing. And, of course, people of all ages can come and work on whatever they're doing in peace and quiet. Most people don't have homes big enough to have a study! Libraries are a basic public provision, like electricity and water and your GP.

How would you encourage the reading habit in young people?

The problem is that kids come to think of reading as a chore when they are set books at school. They associate it with exams and essays and grades. That has its place, but if you want to open their minds to what reading really has to offer, you have to persuade them that it's the opposite of a chore – it's a form of liberation.

Once you present reading as a choice rather than a duty, things can change. It doesn't matter if you're reading Dickens or Lee Child, it's all good. The habit is what counts. It's brain food. And it's also a good way of encouraging kids to approach what they see and read critically – reading a good book can give you the antibodies you need against people telling you how to think and behave. Books are freedom.

Do you think there's a similar problem with Shakespeare?

Yes, that's another good example. The plays were written for everyone, to be enjoyed in quite a raucous way. But that's not how they're seen today – they're presented as these incredibly complex, intellectual texts. Well, they are. But they are also meant to be enjoyed and experienced as explorations of universal human experience. They're often very funny.

I only did one Shakespearean part, but it was a very happy experience. It was a TV version of *Hamlet* back in 1964, done by the BBC with Danish radio, and shot at Elsinore itself. Christopher Plummer played the prince, my friend Robert Shaw was Claudius, and Donald Sutherland came on board as Fortinbras. I played Horatio. I think the BBC still show it occasionally. I loved doing it.

Mind you, I once heard John Wayne reading 'To be, or not to be' at a charity event – and he stopped after a bit and said, 'Who wrote this shit?'

You love your family, your community of friends and colleagues and your country. How much does Englishness matter to you?

Very much, and it always has. My kind of Englishness is generous, proud and traditional but open to change, old-fashioned but at ease with modern life, and serious when it has to be, but always underpinned by humour.

English people are natural eccentrics and comics. They see the lighter side of absolutely everything and enjoy the absurdities of life. This is the only country in the world that could have produced the Goons, or Tony Hancock, or Peter Cook or the Pythons.

At the same time, we have an incredible history and heritage to share. It's no accident that England has had so few revolutionary uprisings, because it has such a great tradition of adaptation – gradual progress, slower at some moments than others, but in the right direction. I like the welcoming face of England. The big change in my lifetime has been the idea that everyone, at least in theory, can enjoy all the benefits of life here, and we've got to do more to make that a reality.

Patriotism for all, in other words?

Well, if it's not for everyone, then it's hardly patriotism, is it? I've always loved it when young people use the Union Jack in fashion or culture, or you see the flag of St George being waved during an international football tournament – by people from all backgrounds. It's something for everyone to share, and it shouldn't be misused by racist groups.

Do you think there is a growing tendency to dehumanise people who are different?

It's always been there. When we were in Korea, the enemy were referred to as 'gooks', which was just a way of making it psychologically possible to fight them. Because obviously they were just ordinary men like us, with families, and lots of love in their lives. But war stops you from seeing the other side as human beings.

And today?

Well, it's probably worse in some ways, in the sense that the rhetoric now can get so heated, sometimes dangerously so. Whatever issue you're dealing with, at home or abroad, you have to treat people as human beings. That's rule number one. It's my starting point to get along with people in life, not to seek out conflict. I had a bit of anger in me as a young man, but now I just want there to be peace.

During the riots in August 2024, you posted two words on X/ Twitter: 'Calm down'. That post was viewed by more than three million people and was picked up by the press. I know anecdotally that it meant a lot to many people. Why did you do that?

First thing to say is, I'm not a politician. I was responding as a father and a grandfather and a citizen to all the terrible violence that was going on in cities and neighbourhoods around the country.

There had been an absolutely awful tragedy with three little girls being murdered at a holiday dance club in Southport. It was just unbearable. And then suddenly things got out of control, with all sorts of irresponsible rumours and fabrications flying around and people taking to the streets to attack others, burn things down and make life impossible for the police. It was senseless and very un-British.

So all I meant was what I said: it was time for everyone to calm down. I'm deeply opposed to violence and this was just unacceptable. If the tweet had an impact, that's good. I intervene like that extremely rarely, but I felt I had a responsibility to do so.

Responsibility is something you often talk about. Why so?

Again, background has a lot to do with it. You're taught to take responsibility for yourself and, crucially, for others, too.

I was the elder of two brothers, so it was natural for me to respond to that. I'm not a control freak, but I do feel a deep sense of responsibility to my loved ones.

My younger brother Stanley passed away in 2013. Amazingly, after our mum died, we discovered that we had an older half-brother called David, who had been living in mental institutions and nursing homes for more than fifty years without us having the slightest idea that he existed.

It turned out that Mum had visited him secretly every Monday, taking chocolates and sweets, and that she had made every nurse swear on the Bible that they would never reveal his identity. I did my best to make life more comfortable for David before he died in 1992. But what really struck me was how my mum had kept up her visits for all those years with none of us ever guessing.

I was so proud of her for never wavering in her responsibility to, and love for, her first child, even though she couldn't see him every day. It was an unexpected life lesson – and one very much in line with the values that she had taught us as we were growing up.

Do you think people run away from responsibility in the modern world?

It's hard to generalise, as you see people every day doing the most amazing things for one another. What has frayed a bit is what I would call social responsibility: the sense of looking out for your neighbours and checking up, as a matter of course, on your friends. As high streets have declined, people bump into each less often out at the shops. There are fewer physical spaces where communities meet all the time. People tend to live more and more in their bubbles.

But we have to figure all this out, don't we? People are living longer and longer, housing is getting more expensive and the multigenerational household is becoming more common again. Isolation is not really practical or desirable.

True, and I hope there are clever policy people working on answers to all that. One general way of addressing it is to mention how I always answer another question. Whenever people used to ask me where I was going on holiday, I'd say, 'Home.'

Being with my family at home is the best holiday ever. We'd travel together when I was filming, but it wasn't the same as being at home, out in the garden, watching Oscar 'screeners' together – one of our winter rituals, at the time of year when Academy members are sent all the top films to watch for voting. It used to be DVDs, though now they upload them online with password protection. We love watching movies together in our home cinema.

What I'm really saying is that the answer today is, in essence, the same as it's always been. The world of 2024 may look transformed, but it will be held together and improved by the same things that have always worked. Responsibility, decency, cool tempers, a sense of humour, and stretching a hand of friendship out to those who need a bit of help. Not in order to trap them in dependency, but to make it possible for those that can to get back on their feet. It really isn't a complicated formula.

Though simple doesn't mean easy?

No, and this is the nub of it all. Ditching old social habits can be a mistake. When I was acting, I always used Stanislavski's idea of 'sense memory': if you wanted to evoke a particular emotion, you'd dive into a memory, whether joyful or painful. I could use this technique to cry on demand! It's a powerful tool.

I guess society needs its own 'sense memory', too – not to fake emotions but to nudge us into strengthening and reviving past habits, to remember how to behave, how to be courteous, how to rub along with people.

We are surrounded by technology and a culture that often seems to encourage us to be horrible to each other, not to listen to each other, and to get as worked up as we can about trivia. All for cheap thrills. That's no good at all.

Manners, politeness and thoughtfulness are what make the world go round, and they always have been. However many wars and horrendous conflicts there have been, in the end human beings have no choice but to get along. It doesn't always pan out, but that's the objective.

And it's important for everyone to remember that, in matters great and small. Before you speak, ask whether you have anything to contribute to the conversation beyond rage or resentment. Before you post that mean tweet, take a breath and ask, is it really worth it? Who might I be hurting? Why am I even doing this?

The right to speak your mind is precious, but it is not the same as the obligation to act like an idiot. My strong advice? Don't confuse the two.

I am so grateful to my fans. But nothing matters more than being with Shakira.

11

When One Door Closes . . . Another Opens

You're not inclined to nostalgia, are you?

No, not at all. I've lived my life looking forward and it's served me well. There are a couple of exceptions. I miss family and friends who have passed on, and I try to honour their memory.

Also, I am happy to document my past, as I've done in memoirs and films like *My Generation*. I enjoy doing it, and it seems to have an audience, which is great.

But that's absolutely not the same as being stuck in the past, which happens all too easily to people once they've passed a certain age. Not me. I love thinking about what's going on today and what might be coming down the track. It's much more exciting.

I heard the director Jeff Nichols, who made The Bikeriders *(2023), say that nostalgia is fine as long as it includes a recognition that you can't revisit or recreate the past.*

That sounds like a good attitude. You can remember the past with fondness, but you should never get trapped in it. What's the point? You can't bring it back and you certainly can't change the mistakes you made. It's an error to fret over the things you got wrong, anyway. The trick is to learn from them and move on.

You can't step into the same river twice, right?

Exactly. And would you even want to? I mean, all you have is today and the opportunities it presents. The past can play a part in your wisdom, but it shouldn't be a sort of dusty manual that you consult all the time, tut-tutting at what's going on in the modern world. That's totally wrong.

How do you focus on today and tomorrow, rather than yesterday?

Well, acting is all about the moment, so actors are hardwired to live in it, or they should be. As a way of life, it gives you a kind of focus that helps you seize the day in everything else. I always say that life is not a rehearsal. We only get one life – or at least that's what I believe, I know others believe in reincarnation! – and it is just common sense to treat every day as a gift and make the most of it.

That's living in the present. What about the future?

There's obviously only a limited extent to which we can know what's coming down the line. If we'd been having this conversation in the year 2000, would we have predicted things like 9/11, the financial crash, Covid, the Ukraine war, politics going nuts? It's impossible to forecast very much, especially now with technology shifting the goalposts all the time.

What counts is the way in which you face the future. In my case, that's always been about optimism. I accept that things don't always work out, but I look to the future on the basis that life will get better and better.

For whom?

That's unknowable, too! I hope for more and more people, all over the world. I hope that wealth-creators continue to be encouraged so that it's possible for more and more people to escape poverty and to achieve a better standard of living.

I hope that all the incredible medical breakthroughs that are happening benefit everyone and not just folk who can afford to go private. I'm in favour of private healthcare, as it relieves the NHS of a certain burden. But if, say, cancer is cured, I want everyone to benefit from that miracle, rather than just the rich.

Do you believe in God?

Yes, I do. I was in the choir when I was a little boy, and when I was young, in North Runcton, I was in church every Sunday and I knew the vicar. I've always trusted in God and, when you think of what I've become, I don't think he's done badly for me. I like to think that if God had a voice, he'd sound like John Huston!

How important is that belief to your optimism?

They go hand in hand. I have had such an incredibly fortunate life that I can't see any other explanation. The great middle-weight Rocky Graziano wrote a book called *Somebody Up There Likes Me* (1955), which is exactly how I feel.

My beliefs are personal rather than especially religious. I'm not talking about going to church every Sunday. My dad was a Catholic, my mum was a Protestant, and my wife is a Muslim. Jane Russell once took me to a Christian Science lunch!

Nobody has a monopoly on God and there all sorts of ways of believing. Mind you, I'm not too sure about the idea of the 'meek inheriting the earth'. My whole battle in life was not to be meek but to stand up for myself!

My beliefs are more to do with the idea of a divine presence guiding events and in a basically benign way. I would never dream of imposing them on anybody else, that would be terrible. But, personally, I think it is the only way of making sense of the universe. I talk to God every day.

What do you say to him?

I say to him, 'I'll have fish and chips!'

The great fish and chip shop in the sky! What about people who don't believe in God? Where do they get their sense of right and wrong?

It comes from your upbringing, no question. What you see around you, what you learn is acceptable and not acceptable, the morals that your family teaches you. That's why it's so important for young people to have good role models, teachers and guides in life, in addition to their relatives. But it's important to insist that there is such a thing as right and wrong, and the sooner people learn it, the better.

What do you think of people's preoccupation today with 'downtime'?

It's just another word for 'taking it easy', isn't it? I'm all for taking it easy, in the sense that everyone needs to recharge their batteries from time to time. And everyone should spend time with their family, which is why I always took mine with me when I was filming. I'm not so keen on the idea of doing nothing as a sort of entitlement. It's not a good use of a life and it will make you miserable sooner than you think.

I always say to young actors, 'Don't make great spaces in your life.' In other words, don't confuse taking a break, which is important, with idleness, which is terrible. The longer you sit around doing nothing, the harder it will be to get going again. It's one of the worst habits a person can slip into and it's an occupational hazard in acting, when you never know when the next job is coming.

If you have spare time, use it to your advantage to learn something new or acquire a new skill. It's a good rule in life that you'll only regret the things you didn't do.

What do you make of what medicine can do nowadays?

I think it's incredible. I had an operation for spinal stenosis a couple of years ago and I'm not as mobile as I once was. But it's amazing what surgery and physiotherapy can achieve now, as I have discovered. Look at how quickly they got the vaccine up and running during the pandemic. It was extraordinary.

Remember that I was in my twenties before general polio vaccination started in this country – that had taken ages to be perfected. The pace of medical science today is breathtaking. My 'celestial twin' Quincy Jones has always said to me, 'If you live another five years, they'll discover so many things you'll live another five.' I like his way of thinking!

Any diet or fitness tips for people seeking to live a long life?

All the basics: avoid sugar and salt, eat gluten-free bread, grow your own veg, drink in moderation, don't smoke, exercise in any way you can. I'm in two minds about health foods. The people who work in health foods stores always look so unwell.

When it comes to staying in shape, you don't have to be Arnold Schwarzenegger or run a marathon. All movement is good, anything that keeps your muscles busy is good. A little and often is better than exhausting yourself once a week. I used to walk a lot, but now I get lots of physio. It's a really important part of my routine.

When I was in my twenties, I lived on booze and cigarettes. Your attitude can remain as youthful as you like, but your body has an age attached to it, like the mileage in a car, and you should act accordingly. You don't have to live like a puritan, and you should certainly have treats. But the better you take care of yourself, the more fun you'll be able to have.

As a former soldier, have you been shocked by the conflicts that have erupted in the last few years?

Yes. Very much so. Having lived through the Second World War and fought in Korea, I had really hoped that this century would be more peaceful than it has been. I didn't foresee a land war in Europe or such bloodshed in the Middle East, all these years later.

The thriller I wrote, *Deadly Game*, was primarily meant to be an entertainment, but it also reflected that heightened sense of risk. Today's kids don't face conscription or even National Service. But they do doomscroll on their phones and see daily images and clips of terrible violence in Ukraine and Israel and Gaza. That can't be good for them.

I played tough guys many times, but I'm not like that at all in real life. I come from the first generation that really demanded peace, and we're still waiting. I truly hope that these conflicts are resolved very soon and that the world can focus on jaw-jaw rather than war-war. The last century was so violent. I hope with all my heart that this one won't be the same. But there's no way of knowing whether it will or not. That's an anxiety I *do* have.

But you are very optimistic about the younger generation itself, aren't you?

Enormously so. My grandkids have transformed the way I see the world. It's endlessly exciting to talk to them and hear about what they've been up to and what they'd like to do with their lives. They've put on shows for us at Christmas, they're always coming up with new things. I think they'll be an incredible generation.

In what way?

Too soon to be specific! But they have an energy and an urgency that is just wonderful to see. They are children of this century, they understand it all instinctively. And they want to make something of themselves, whatever that may be.

They try their hands at different things and different skills, which is a terrific attitude to have. I think parents who try to force their children into a particular career are missing the point. That's not your job at all. Your job is to provide your kids with all the love and support and wisdom that you can.

When I see somebody trying to make one of their children a doctor or a lawyer or whatever, it's so obvious that they're trying to act out their own ambitions. That's not what parenting is about. It's not about you. It's about *them*.

All this generational change that's brewing – it reminds me a lot of the spirit of the Sixties. Of course, they will all have to figure out exactly what form it takes for themselves – you can't predict it. And it will probably be lots of things, rather than one big thing.

Do you worry about them?

Oh, of course, but that's just the natural protective instinct of a grandfather. I worry about the world and what it's going to be like for them. It's obviously going to be very different.

That's the sort of anxiety that anyone with responsibilities has about their family. But I have great faith in them and their ability to work out what to do and how to get on. I think there is great change coming, and their generation will do wonderful things.

What do you make of the anxiety and mental health problems that a lot of young people suffer from nowadays?

Well, personally, I've never been much of a believer in psychiatrists or psychotherapy. But that's just my opinion. People should seek help wherever they need to. There's never any shame in asking for assistance.

What I would say is that a lot of the anxiety people feel today is probably avoidable. For a start, they should stop valuing themselves in comparison to others all the time. Social media is terrible in that way – all this nonsense about getting 'likes' or whatever it is. It's completely artificial, worrying about nothing.

The opinion of others *can* bolster your self-esteem, but it should never, ever be its basis. Was it nice to get my Oscars? Of course it was. But I never judged my performances by awards or what the critics said. I knew whether I'd done the part justice or not. I was competing with myself, not with others. I wanted to be the best actor I could be, not the best actor in the world – whatever that means!

I think young people's mental health difficulties wouldn't be so bad if they paid a bit less attention to everyone else's judgements and concentrated on their own set of values. Who cares what somebody online says about you? They might not even be a real person.

The thing to do – and it might take a while – is to really think long and hard about what matters to *you*, what things you believe in, what skills you want to perfect. Take stock as often as you can and ask: how am I doing compared to six months ago? Have I achieved any of my goals? Or am I closer to achieving any of them? If not, what changes should I make to make that more likely?

Nobody but you can answer those questions. Ask your mentors and teachers for advice, of course. That's a given. But, in the end, you have to be honest with yourself. That's a good path to a contented life. Worrying all the time about what other people think is a recipe for just the opposite. What would they know, after all?

A lot has changed socially since the Sixties, hasn't it? Feminism wasn't really a transformative force until the Seventies.

That's true, although women played a much bigger part in the Sixties than is sometimes recognised. You had Mary Quant, Twiggy, Jean Shrimpton, Marianne Faithfull, Jane Fonda, Shirley MacLaine, Vanessa Redgrave and lots of others. They were just as important as the guys. And the fashion was all about women dressing exactly as they wanted, not having to conform to old-fashioned stereotypes.

Remember where we'd all come from. A world where the men were in charge of the family, but the women did all the work in the house, all the laundry and everything, bathing the kids, looking after the kids, taking the kids to school. And now women were saying: actually, we want careers of our own, we want equal pay, we want to be stars, too. It was all part of the spirit of change.

And you made your position on apartheid very clear in your work with Sidney Poitier. What do you make of the social justice movements today?

I am not a natural campaigner and I'm certainly not a political activist. I have helped out with particular issues and charities along the way, but I don't see my role as being a political voice.

What is true is that I will always do my best to represent the underdog – Quincy Jones always used to say to me that cockney rhyming slang was like black American dialect, which I thought was very interesting. The working class in this country never faced actual slavery, but it definitely experienced servitude.

I can't bear it when I read about children going hungry. That's why I recently announced my support for Magic Breakfast, which is a great charity that arranges breakfasts for kids and campaigns to prevent morning hunger. It's such an important issue. I've supported the NSPCC for many years, too.

People still trust movie stars and their sporting heroes, like Marcus Rashford, who campaigned successfully for free school meals during the pandemic. But, in general, trust is plummeting.

Is that right? That's not good. It's hard for anything to work without trust.

Yes. Politicians, media, most institutions, even scientists are much less trusted than they used to be.

Trust has to be earned. The media blow it when they stir things up or sensationalise everything. Politicians blow it by looking as though they are in it for themselves and are all the same.

Do you think they are?

Maybe not all of them, but those that are honourable and really care about the public have a huge job ahead of them to win back the voters' trust. I wouldn't like to be in their shoes.

What do you think about 'political correctness'?

People often ask me this. My view is what it's always been. You should treat everyone, no matter what class, religion, race, sex or sexuality they are, as *you* would like to be treated, with decency and courtesy. That's pretty core to my beliefs. I can't stand bigotry, racism and prejudice. Take people as you find them and learn how to get along with them.

You talk about big change coming as the younger generation finds its feet. How do older people fit in to big cultural moments like that? Are they left on the shelf?

Not at all. Take my mum – she didn't feel she'd been left on the shelf in the Sixties for a second. She was happy that I was doing well and enjoyed it when I showed her round, in London and Beverly Hills. I remember having tea in LA with David Hockney and his mum and the two mothers were chatting away like they would have been in England! It was great.

So I don't think it's anything to worry about. New movements in art and fashion and music and technology are exciting, and it's fun to see it all happening. Part of the pleasure of life is realising that there is always new stuff coming down the track. Some people get stuck in their own youth and resent everything that comes after, and that's a really silly tangle to get caught up in. Was the Sixties the greatest decade ever? Well, of course, my generation tends to think so. But that doesn't mean there won't be better decades.

Your movie with Alan Arkin and Morgan Freeman, Going in Style *(2017), was a celebration of getting older, wasn't it?*

It was, and it was a real romp. It was actually a remake by Zach Braff of a 1979 movie that had starred George Burns, Art Carney and Lee Strasberg. We played three retired working-class guys who are lifelong pals and find that their pensions have been ripped off by the corporations and the bank. And they decide to become bank robbers, just for one day. Ann-Margret was in the movie, too, as Alan's love interest.

It was a hoot doing all the chase sequences in New York and we had a lot of fun. I found a house in Sands Point on the beach not far from the shoot and the whole family stayed with me for seven weeks. What could be better? It was the happiest movie experience I ever had.

The film doesn't take itself too seriously – it's a caper, essentially – but the idea was that older people can still take a stand against injustice and take control of their destiny. I liked that very much.

Also, Alan could never remember his lines. He had them all written on the wall. At the end of the picture, there was a shot on a bridge overlooking the river and Alan was in it. I was looking round for where his lines were – on a tree or something. Anyway, I looked over the edge of the bridge and there was a little fella holding up a board with the lines on! Hilarious. He was a lovely guy, Alan, and he gave a tremendous performance. He passed away last year, sadly.

Has moviemaking helped you keep up with changes in the world?

Yes, and in lots of ways. I've watched amazing technical innovation in moviemaking, especially in my films with Chris Nolan. It's a perfect example of using technology for human purposes, in this case the art of film. But I've also enjoyed the opportunities that being older brings you to keep in touch with the world if you want to.

What happens is, you go from being a star to being a leading actor. A star makes sure that the movie fits him. A leading actor fits into the movie. And, actually, the parts can be more interesting.

A good example is one of the last films I acted in, which was called *Best Sellers* (2021). The director was excellent, Lina Roessler – one to watch. I play this grumpy old writer called Harris Shaw, who had one great success with a novel and then didn't publish anything at all for fifty years. Harris is so bad-tempered – the first thing he says in the movie is when he answers the phone: 'He's dead, bugger off!'

Aubrey Plaza plays the daughter of Harris's original publisher, who's trying to keep his company alive. So, to her great surprise, I hand over the manuscript of a new novel and the film is a sort of road movie about these two characters going on a book tour and trying to make sense of their lives. Aubrey was very good in the movie. I remember her telling me how nervous she was on the first day, but we got on great. We all used to have dinner together and it was a very enjoyable shoot.

I saw that she and the rest of the cast got a standing ovation at Cannes this year for their performances in the new Francis Ford Coppola movie. That's one of the great things about being an actor for many years. You get to work with all the rising talents as well as your heroes. It's a very exciting way to experience a career.

Stardom works differently now, doesn't it? What do you make of the Taylor Swift phenomenon?

Yes, stardom is definitely different to the era of say, John Wayne, Humphrey Bogart, Elizabeth Taylor. People's attention is more divided than it used to be, there's more competition from all sorts of directions. There's not the really the sense there used to be of the big cultural event of the week. So there are definitely fewer actors and musicians whose name alone can guarantee a movie or a record will make money.

But stardom is still stardom. Tom Cruise is amazing, he'd have been a star in any era. His performance in the closing ceremony of the Paris Olympics was just stunning, the whole world watching as he carried the Olympic flag. Nobody else could have done that.

And I think Taylor Swift is incredible, a giant star. You know she was a country singer to start with? And now she fills stadiums all over the world, with audiences of 100,000, and politicians are desperate for her to support them. That's extraordinary.

You can just tell how much hard work lies behind what she's achieved, too. It's no accident. She has really earned her success and it hasn't come overnight. She's down-to-earth, which is almost always part of it. Not spoiled by all the accolades and money. That's impressive.

We talked earlier about there being more auditions in life today. Are there any lessons from acting in that respect?

It's an interesting question. There are all sorts of things that acting teaches you that can translate into real life.

One I have thought about a lot is the art of keeping your eyes open. I mean literally so, not blinking. I discovered that this was very powerful in movie acting, because your face is enormous up there on the screen and if your eyes remain open it commands the audience's attention. It works in real life, too. Not blinking – if you can do it! – is a way of maximising your presence and making people listen to you.

The same with your voice. Early on in my movie career, when I was waiting for production to begin on *Gambit*, I bumped into John Wayne in the lobby of the Beverly Hills Hotel and he was very complimentary about my work. He said, 'Talk low, talk slow, and don't say too much.' And I took that on board – obviously! What I found out is that powerful people talk slowly and less powerful people talk fast. So you can convey confidence in any setting by speaking at a relaxed pace, as if you have no intention of letting anyone dictate the speed at which you say what you have to say. It sends a subliminal message.

Is it possible to live a solitary life and still be fulfilled?

It may be, but I couldn't do it. My life has been defined by my relationships with other people – especially Shakira. I always say that there are three secrets to a long and happy marriage: love, separate bathrooms, and knowing your spouse's work. Well, Shakira acted in *The Man Who Would Be King* – so that's all three! It's an equal partnership. I have been unbelievably lucky to spend my life with her. We're both strong and stubborn and we have been so happy together!

I have my daughters Niki and Natasha, and no father could be prouder. And then, when I was seventy-six, along came grandchildren. It felt like my world had been completed.

How important in life is courage?

It's definitely important, and it can express itself in many ways. My mum was courageous when she took care of us after my dad went off to war. My dad was courageous when he was fighting – though, like many of his generation, he never really talked about it. And he was courageous in the way that he worked so hard, day after day, getting up at 4 a.m., without giving it a second thought. That's character.

I think everyone, sooner or later, faces a challenge that tests their courage. There will probably be many, but the first is the one that counts most. For me, it was in Korea when we were out on patrol and thought we were going to die. And we all agreed that, if this was really the end, we were going to 'die dear' or 'die expensive'.

What did that mean?

It meant that the enemy would pay a heavy price, even if he took us all out. It's a good principle in life. You never know when your number's up, but you don't go down without a fight.

I had been quite shy when I was growing up, but in Korea I realised that I could stand up for myself. I hadn't known that about myself before. The circumstances were extreme – I wouldn't wish them on anyone – but the lesson was a valuable one. I was never really frightened again. I'd stared death in the face, after all.

Is courage a component of optimism?

There's a difference between being courageous and being fool-hardy. You can't be successful without taking risks. But you shouldn't be reckless, especially when other people depend upon you. Courage is useful because it's all about recognising fear and understanding it, which enables you to move forward in a positive way.

What does that involve?

Well, fear is natural, it's part of being human. Courage is the right response to it, which means doing what has to be done. Recklessness is when you take stupid risks that might harm others.

And when one door closes . . .

. . . another door opens. I retired from acting in the same year that I became a thriller writer. Who knows what I might try next?

It's all about moving forward, isn't it?

Absolutely. Look, I'm ninety-one. In ten years, I'll be a hundred and one. I've got the Olympics in 2028 to prepare for.

That's a lot of training.

It is. But I like to keep busy.

You do. So – no regrets?

Oh no, there's too much to celebrate and too much to look forward to. Great times lie ahead, you just wait.

In the meantime, any bits of advice you'd like to mention?

Wherever possible, get someone else to do your stunts.

Very helpful. Anything else?

Yes. Don't look back, you'll trip over.

MICHAEL ACCORDING TO HIS FRIENDS AND COLLEAGUES

CHRISTOPHER NOLAN

I cast him in every film just as an example to everyone else. He's just a lovely guy to be around.

SHIRLEY MACLAINE

He tickled me with his dry, sardonic wit ... Michael is the actor who works more than any other in our business. He takes a part and finds a laugh in every corner. I'm so glad he never forgot his humble beginnings, because that memory is the reason for the audience's continued identifications with him.

QUINCY JONES

I hear his name, I see his movies, I get a call from him, it always touches me from the bottom of my soul.

BRIAN DE PALMA (director of *Dressed to Kill*)

I was very fortunate . . . Michael's a delight to work with. He's very witty, he's very bright.

JOHN HUSTON (director of *The Man Who Would Be King*)

[Michael and Sean Connery] couldn't have been better to work with. Many of the scenes were between just the two of them, and they rehearsed together at night. Together they worked up each scene so well beforehand that all I had to decide was how best to shoot it. It was like watching a polished vaudeville act – everything on cue, and perfect timing.

LEWIS GILBERT

He took me down to the East End of London . . . and we went to a tailor where we got him all the kind of clothes that Alfie would have worn and suddenly he started to put these clothes on and he strutted round this shop – and he was Alfie.

OLIVER STONE

One of the best raconteurs I have ever heard.

SIR LAURENCE OLIVIER (during the filming of *Sleuth*)

I thought I had an assistant. I see I have a partner.

JULIE WALTERS

There was talk of doing [*Educating Rita*] with Paul Newman and Dolly Parton. But then Michael Caine came on board as Frank and I was in . . . Michael was lovely, so generous to me.

SYLVESTER STALLONE (on filming *Escape to Victory* with Michael)

What a butt-kicking I got!

SIR BEN KINGSLEY

There's not an atom of fear in his body, he's therefore spontaneous . . . You know, rather like watching an opera singer as they go up the scale, he's going to hit that note, his voice isn't going to crack, or watching a tightrope walker, he's not going to wobble on the rope. It's that wonderful quality.

ZACH BRAFF (director of *Going in Style*)

Sir Michael Caine tweets like he's making an announcement on a microphone to a large crowd. Listen to the living legend!

QUENTIN TARANTINO

I'd love to work with Michael Caine. I've always been a huge Michael Caine fan, I think he's absolutely terrific.

ROGER MOORE

It was around mid-1964, I was walking across Piccadilly, and coming towards me were two actors: one was Terence Stamp and the other was a bespectacled, tall, good-looking blond chap, whom I'd seen the night before in a TV play written by Johnny Speight.

'You're going to be a big star,' I dared to say to the blond actor.

'Fuck me! Roger Moore!' he replied. His name was Michael Caine. He was indeed to become a big star.

LINA ROESSLER (director of *Best Sellers*)

I think what makes him so great is that he is such a genuine, authentic, humble, generous human being. So that translates into his work as an actor. To be so open. To be ready and available to give and receive.

BOB HOSKINS

He's got poetry dripping out of his soul.

BONUS EXTRAS

Michael's Cooking Tips

Cooking steak

Cook in a pan, with butter and oil, and keep basting with butter and oil from the pan. Important: rest for eight minutes before you serve.

Two-chicken roast

- 2 chickens
- Rosemary
- Thyme
- Garlic
- Salt and pepper
- A lemon
- Olive oil
- Carrots, sliced
- Celery, sliced
- A chicken stock cube
- 1 tablespoon cranberry sauce
- 1 tablespoon cornflour
- White wine

1. Preheat the oven to 200°C/400°F/gas mark 6.
2. Remove chickens from fridge – must be room temperature.
3. Put rosemary, thyme, garlic, salt and pepper in the cavities of the chickens then half of lemon in each.
4. Put olive oil over the chickens.
5. Prepare your baking pan with slices of carrots, celery and chicken stock cube with 200ml hot water.
6. Put chickens on their backs in the pan and roast for 1hr 30 minutes.
7. Baste the chickens twice.
8. Pierce the legs of the chickens with a skewer – if they're done, the juice will be golden and clear.
9. Take them out, put in a warm dish, cover with parchment paper, then silver foil, and rest for 30 minutes before serving.

Gravy: To the juice, sliced carrots and celery in the baking pan, add herbs, one tablespoon of cranberry sauce, and one tablespoon of cornflour dissolved in water. Crush everything. Add some white wine, then strain in a colander sieve. Taste and add pepper or salt.

Roast beef

- Roll of beef
- Carrots, sliced
- Celery, sliced
- Onions, chopped
- Black pepper
- Rosemary

- A bay leaf
- Red wine
- A meat stock cube

1. Tip: keep your cooking utensils for the beef in a separate drawer.
2. Choose your roll of beef.
3. Preheat the oven to 200°C/400°F/gas mark 6.
4. Put in a baking pan, with slices of carrots, celery, chopped onions.
5. Add black pepper, rosemary, bay leaf and 150ml water.
6. Time of cooking for every kilo: 15 minutes.
7. Put in the oven for 15 minutes plus appropriate time per kilo.
8. Baste the meat with gravy from the pan.
9. When it's cooked, rest for 45 minutes on a platter, covered with silver foil and a kitchen towel.

Gravy: Add red wine to the pan, then a meat stock cube melted in hot water and crushed.
Put gravy through colander sieve, add pepper and salt, then heat.

Bread and butter pudding

- Large knob of butter
- 10 slices of medium white sliced bread, crusts removed
- 2 bananas, sliced
- 50g/2oz sultanas
- 3 eggs

- 4 tablespoons sugar
- 570ml/1 pint full-fat milk
- 4 drops vanilla essence
- 2 generous tablespoons rum
- Cream or vanilla ice cream to go on top

1. Preheat the oven to 150°C/300°F/gas mark 2. All you need is an ovenproof dish, a spoon, and a mixing bowl to prepare this dish.
2. It's a good idea to make it in advance if you're cooking for guests.
3. Prepare an ovenproof dish by greasing it with butter. Place the bread, having buttered several slices, in layers between the sliced bananas and sultanas.
4. Beat the eggs in with the sugar and add the milk. Then add the vanilla essence and rum.
5. Pour the mixture over the bread and butter and leave it, covered with clingfilm or foil, for one hour in the fridge. Bake, uncovered, for 45 minutes. Then let it rest for an hour to improve.
6. Serve in warmed bowls with double cream or good-quality vanilla ice cream.

P.S. Use the butter's wrapper for greasing the dish as this will save on kitchen paper.

Baked potatoes (this is Natasha's, actually)

1. Preheat the oven to 220°C/425°F/gas mark 7.
2. Wash the potatoes then dry thoroughly.
3. Prick all over with a fork.

4. Smear with olive oil and sea salt.
5. Place in microwave for 10 minutes.
6. Place in preheated oven and cook for an hour.

Roast potatoes (this is mine)

• Potatoes
• A bunch of rosemary
• 2 cloves garlic
• Olive oil
• Celery salt

1. Preheat the oven to 180°C/350°F/gas mark 4.
2. Go for Maris Piper or Mayan Gold potatoes.
3. Soak a bunch of rosemary and two cloves of garlic in a baking tin of olive oil. N.B. The oil must be at room temperature when you put it in the baking tray.
4. Boil the potatoes for 10 minutes (only 5 for the Mayan Golds).
5. Strain and dry.
6. Dry the saucepan and tip the potatoes back in – give them a really good shake until they are fluffy.
7. Take the rosemary and garlic out of the oil and replace with the potatoes.
8. Sprinkle with celery salt and place in a preheated oven for 1hr 30 minutes (1hr for the Mayan Golds).

Cook with turmeric – It's great for the memory!

Michael's Ultimate Chill-out Mix

- No Ordinary Morning – Chicane
- Café de Flore – Doctor Rockit
- Silence – Delerium ft. Sarah McLachlan
- Summertime – Wass ft. Earl T
- Lay Lady Lay – Magnet ft. Gemma Hayes
- Sinnerman – Nina Simone
- Rose Rouge – St Germain
- Sunshine's Better – John Martyn
- Path of Love – Atman
- Crossing – Agartha
- Everytime – Lustral
- Spiritual High (State of Independence) – Moodswings ft. Chrissie Hynde
- Jupiter – Craig Pruess
- Swollen – Bent
- Street Tattoo – Stan Getz
- Hurry to Me – Roy Budd
- Fields of Gold – Eva Cassidy
- Move Closer – Phyllis Nelson

Michael's *Desert Island Discs*

Viva La Vida – Coldplay

One Day Like This – Elbow

Variations on an Original Theme, Op. 36: Variation IX
'Nimrod' – Edward Elgar

No Ordinary Morning – Chicane

Swollen – Bent

Move Closer – Phyllis Nelson

My Way – Frank Sinatra (*Castaway's favourite*)

Happy Christmas (War is Over) – John Lennon & the Plastic
Ono Band

BOOK CHOICE: *The Fountainhead* – Ayn Rand

LUXURY CHOICE: A large bed with 50 per cent goose down
pillows.

First broadcast on BBC Radio 4, Christmas Day, 2009.

Michael's Top Humphrey Bogart Movies

1. *Casablanca* (dir. Michael Curtiz, 1942)
2. *The Treasure of the Sierra Madre* (dir. John Huston, 1948)
3. *The Maltese Falcon* (dir. John Huston, 1941)
4. *The Caine Mutiny* (dir. Edward Dmytryk, 1954)
5. *The African Queen* (dir. John Huston, 1951)
6. *The Petrified Forest* (dir. Archie Mayo, 1936)
7. *Key Largo* (dir. John Huston, 1948)
8. *The Big Sleep* (dir. Howard Hawks, 1946)

Prime Ministers During Michael's Lifetime (So Far)

1. Ramsay MacDonald was already PM when Michael was born in March 1933 and stood down in June 1935 (the two events were unrelated)
2. Stanley Baldwin (June 1935–May 1937)
3. Neville Chamberlain (May 1937–May 1940)
4. Winston Churchill (May 1940–July 1945 *and* October 1951–April 1955)
5. Clement Attlee (July 1945–October 1951)
6. Anthony Eden (April 1955–January 1957)
7. Harold Macmillan (January 1957–October 1963)
8. Alec Douglas-Home (October 1963–October 1964)
9. Harold Wilson (October 1964–June 1970 *and* March 1974–April 1976)
10. Edward Heath (June 1970–March 1974)
11. James Callaghan (April 1976–May 1979)
12. Margaret Thatcher (May 1979–November 1990)
13. John Major (November 1990–May 1997)
14. Tony Blair (May 1997–June 2007)
15. Gordon Brown (June 2007–May 2010)
16. David Cameron (May 2010–July 2016)
17. Theresa May (July 2016–July 2019)
18. Boris Johnson (July 2019–September 2022)
19. Liz Truss (September 2022–October 2022)
20. Rishi Sunak (October 2022–July 2024)
21. Keir Starmer (July 2024–)

MICHAEL'S GUIDE TO LIFE IN 32 LINES

If you can keep your head when all about you
Are losing theirs and blaming it on you;
If you can trust yourself when all men doubt you,
But make allowance for their doubting too;
If you can wait and not be tired by waiting,
Or, being lied about, don't deal in lies,
Or, being hated, don't give way to hating,
And yet don't look too good, nor talk too wise;

If you can dream – and not make dreams your master;
If you can think – and not make thoughts your aim;
If you can meet with triumph and disaster
And treat those two impostors just the same;
If you can bear to hear the truth you've spoken
Twisted by knaves to make a trap for fools,
Or watch the things you gave your life to broken,
And stoop and build 'em up with worn-out tools;

If you can make one heap of all your winnings
And risk it on one turn of pitch-and-toss,

And lose, and start again at your beginnings
And never breathe a word about your loss;
If you can force your heart and nerve and sinew
To serve your turn long after they are gone,
And so hold on when there is nothing in you
Except the Will which says to them: 'Hold on';

If you can talk with crowds and keep your virtue,
Or walk with kings – nor lose the common touch;
If neither foes nor loving friends can hurt you;
If all men count with you, but none too much;
If you can fill the unforgiving minute
With sixty seconds' worth of distance run –
Yours is the Earth and everything that's in it,
And – which is more – you'll be a Man, my son!

'If—' by Rudyard Kipling, c. 1895

ACKNOWLEDGEMENTS

As so often, I am indebted to the late John Huston, as it was a collection of interviews with him that got me thinking that a book like this might be interesting to do. I am very grateful to Matt d'Ancona for agreeing to work with me on the project.

Caroline Michel – Matt's agent, as well as mine – was, as ever, 100 per cent supportive, and we both thank her.

At Hodder & Stoughton, it was Rowena Webb who first encouraged me to pursue the idea, and Rupert Lancaster who so deftly edited the book: I owe them both a great debt of gratitude.

Thanks, too, are due to Christian Duck, Juliet Brightmore, and the sales, marketing, publicity and production teams at Hodder that made this book possible.

Beverly Hetherington and Jennifer Bird, our transcribers, did a fantastic job. In my office, Teresa Selwyn provided tremendous support and friendship. Special thanks to budding cineaste Teddy d'Ancona for his excellent research on the project.

And – as always, and forever – thank you to my wonderful wife Shakira, who makes everything a joy.

MC

PICTURE
ACKNOWLEDGEMENTS

Chapter openers:
1: Getty Images/Don Smith/Radio Times, 2 and 3: Alamy Stock Photo/Everett Collection Inc., 4: Getty Images/George Rose, 5: Alamy Stock Photo/MediaPunch Inc., 6: Shutterstock/John Knoote/Daily Mail, 7: Alamy Stock Photo/Album, 8: Alamy Stock Photo/Collection Christophel, 9: Alamy Stock Photo / Maximum Film, 10: Shutterstock/John Knoote/Daily Mail, 11: Alamy Stock Photo/PA Images.

Inset pages 1–16:
1 above: Alamy Stock Photo/ScreenProd/Photononstop, 1 below: Alamy Stock Photo/Lebrecht Music & Arts, 2 above left: Alamy Stock Photo/colaimages, 2 above right and 2 below: Alamy Stock Photo/Everett Collection Inc., 3 above: Alamy Stock Photo/Trinity Mirror/Mirrorpix, 3 below: Alamy Stock Photo/Moviestore Collection Ltd., 4 above: Alamy Stock Photo/ TCD/Prod.DB, 5 above: Alamy Stock Photo/Photo12, 5 below: Alamy Stock Photo/Entertainment Pictures, 6 above: Alamy Stock Photo/Landmark Media, 6 below: Alamy Stock Photo/ Cinematic, 7 above: Alamy Stock Photo/Everett Collection Inc.,

ABOUT THE AUTHOR

SIR MICHAEL CAINE CBE has been Oscar-nominated six times, winning his first Academy Award for the 1986 film *Hannah and Her Sisters* and his second in 1999 for *The Cider House Rules*. He has starred in over one hundred films. He was appointed a CBE in 1992 and knighted in 2000 in recognition of his contribution to cinema. His 2018 memoir *Blowing the Bloody Doors Off* was a huge bestseller, and his first thriller – *Deadly Game* – was published to great acclaim in 2023. Married for more than fifty years, with two daughters and three grand-children, he and his wife Shakira live in London.